THE DEATH CAP

Boletus appendiculatus. Ca'n Cueg, 1 de setembre de 1965.

Dijous, 1 de octubre de 1965. As I only saw a large number of Scleroderma and the usual "picornels" on my morning walk round the garden, I decided that I would make a start on the job of transfering the better drawings from the lined sketch book into this, & that I would add more of the background material as I worked, in order to give a rather better idea of the environment, as well as to supply myself with extra detail for the making of finished drawings. Today has been sunny but cold, but there may be a new selection for me by tomorow. Any how, it does not matter, as I still have a great many drawings in the other book which should be transfered to this in due course. I want to make this book look as nice as I can as, once I have a sufficiency of drawings I can use it as a kind of sample book to show to people who want to comission drawings from me. The more I draw the better for my technique in this still unfamiliar medium.

Inocybe jurana. 13 de setembre de 1965. Ca'n Cueg, herbaceous border.

A page from Ruthven's Todd's 1965 illustrated diary, showing mushrooms he found while staying at a friend's house in Pollensa, on the the north-east tip of Mallorca.

The Death Cap

A detective story by R.T. Campbell

Introduced by Peter Main
Annotated by Forbes Gibb

A limited edition of 300, of which this is number 137

First published in this edition in Great Britain in 2013 by Lomax Press,
13 Park Place, Stirling, Stirlingshire, FK7 9JR
Enquiries to info@lomaxpress.co.uk

The Death Cap, frontispiece and figures 1-4 © Christopher Todd, 2013
Ruthven Todd: Writer and Naturalist © Peter Main, 2013
Cover illustration © Rebecca Green, 2013
All other material © Lomax Press, 2013

The Death Cap was first published in June 1946 by John Westhouse
(Publishers) Ltd.

ISBN: 978-0-9560288-8-4

Contents

Editor's Foreword
Forbes Gibb

Lomax Press is proud to reprint, with the kind permission of Christopher Todd, a second volume in the Professor Stubbs series: *The Death Cap*. The detective stories of Ruthven Todd are increasingly difficult to track down in the original editions and the success of our reprint of *Take Thee a Sharp Knife* has encouraged us to continue in our mission to bring these works to a wider and contemporary audience.

The text has been annotated to help the modern reader obtain a sense of time and place, and to provide some insights into Todd's literary influences. Obvious typographical and spelling errors have been corrected, but a number of the more unusual anomalies have been preserved.

I hope that you will enjoy this second adventure in the Stubbs canon in which he displays his usual lack of tact, an apparently unquenchable thirst, and a certain disregard for other people's safety. Information on the first reprint, *Take Thee a Sharp Knife*, and other Lomax Press publications, will be found at www.lomaxpress.co.uk

I would like to acknowledge the following for providing information and relevant permissions to allow this project to come to fruition:

- Christopher Todd, for access to family documents and permission to republish the text of *The Death Cap* and the figures in the introduction.
- Peter Main, for his introduction.
- Rebecca Green, for another atmospheric dustwrapper.
- Michiel van der Lugt, Omnis Partners, for book design and typography.

Lomax Press, Stirling, 2013

Ruthven Todd: Writer and Naturalist
Peter Main

The nature of the man

In an introductory chapter to *Take Thee a Sharp Knife,*[1] I described how Ruthven Todd (real name of R. T. Campbell) came to write his detective novels featuring Professor John Stubbs, and I mentioned that his heart did not lie mainly in the field of fiction writing, but in poetry and art history. But an underlying theme which pops up repeatedly in his writings and correspondence with friends is his profound interest in, and knowledge of, the natural world. His son Christopher, in a preface to the same book, recalls a summer visit to see his father when he was living in the rural surroundings of Martha's Vineyard in the 1950s:

> We spent days on the beach and I was impressed by the way he would go snorkelling, and when finding a scallop on the sea bed would, there and then, drag it up, open its shell with his knife and eat it raw. He showed me unusual shells and the strange horseshoe crabs. He had infinite knowledge of the life of the sea as well as that of the forest. You could always put your entire trust in his finding new mushrooms to eat..

When Todd developed the plots for the Stubbs novels, he always drew on his own experience and expertise, and it is not through any random whim of Todd's that the murder victim in *The Death Cap* is eliminated by poisoning with a lethal variety of mushroom. Todd was a remarkably knowledgeable amateur mycologist, and it is this aspect of his personality that I mainly discuss here, but it should be seen in the context of his fascination with the natural world in general. This can be ascribed to two factors: the circumstances of his early life, and a character trait which involved him in an almost compulsive need to research into the minutiae of any subject which caught his interest.

The instincts of a naturalist were fostered in Ruthven soon after he was born. This derived primarily from his mother Christian who was herself a lover of flowers and animals, and a considerable gardener. She in turn inherited this interest from her mother Gertrude Craik. When Gertrude was not tending the garden in the 25-room Georgian town house that she and her husband James Craik (a senior figure in the legal profession) maintained in Edinburgh, the Craiks would pile into carriages with a retinue of servants, and head for their 'country house' - Hailes House – where Gertrude could indulge her

---

1   Campbell, R.T. (2011) *Take Thee a Sharp Knife.* Stirling: Lomax Press.

horticultural passion and expertise, as well as keeping a wide variety of live-stock and pets ranging from Persian cats to lizards and salamanders. Ruthven was only four years old when Gertrude died, and although he retained some memories of her, he always regretted that he had not known her better. He did at least, following his mother's death in 1954, inherit much of her considerable library of natural history books.

Ruthven's first memory of gathering fungi was in 1917, when he was two or three years old, in the woods next to a holiday house called Dunstaffnage, which Gertrude rented on the edge of the Holy Loch on the west coast of Scotland. There he and his younger brother, supervised by a maid, would gather sphagnum moss and stuff it into pillow-cases, to be sent to the Red Cross for dressing the wounds of soldiers in France. While crawling around, his childish eyes were drawn to the bright red, white-spotted, caps of *Amanita muscaria* (fly agaric) mushrooms which are the familiar toad-stools often illustrated in children's fairy tales. As he grew older, he found both fungi and sea-shells a constant fascination; as far as wild mushrooms are concerned, we must assume that this enthusiasm was monitored by his mother, since he did survive into adulthood. During a family holiday near Selkirk in the Scottish Borders, Ruthven's brother David took a tumble, and Ruthven recalled offering him a giant puffball mushroom as a replacement for his concussed skull.

The Todd family (Ruthven was the oldest of ten children) lived in a large house adjacent to Edinburgh's Royal Botanic Garden. The Todds' own garden was home to a hot-house, cold-house, beehives, smaller gardens which Christian created for the children, and her own rock garden which was populated with many exotica obtained though her cultivation of friendships with the employees of the Botanic Garden. Occasionally, to Christian's confusion, quite unexpected species flowered in the rock garden - introduced surreptitiously by Ruthven's replanting of cuttings pilfered from the Botanic Garden. One of the outhouses was also home to Ruthven's pet crocodile, at least until it became unmanageably large and had to be donated to Edinburgh Zoo, and its place was taken later by a Galapagos turtle which he purchased (quite illegally) for £1 from a drunken sailor at the docks.

Ruthven began to absorb the elements of taxonomic classification at a surprisingly early age. As an eleven year-old, combing the beaches near Cramond on the outskirts of Edinburgh, Ruthven was approached by an old man who was so impressed by Ruthven's knowledge of the Latin names of shells that he invited him for tea and cucumber sandwiches at his home at nearby Dalmeny House. (The old gentleman, it later emerged, was none other than Archibald Philip Primrose, 5th Earl of Rosebery, and ex-Prime Minister of Britain, who was to die a few years later.) Todd remained a keen collector of sea-shells throughout his life, and visitors to his small house in Mallorca during the final years of his life admired the glass-fronted cabinets containing shells of considerable beauty.

Figure 1. Part of Ruthven Todd's shell collection.

This interest in taxonomy embraced fungi too, and had practical benefits in Todd's ability to distinguish the delicious from the just about edible, and from the hallucinogenic or highly poisonous varieties of wild mushroom which make fungi a dangerous area for experimentation. His knowledge was in demand by locals wherever he put down roots – if you wanted to know what was safe to eat, Ruthven Todd was your man. And so in *The Death Cap*, it was natural that Todd chose poisoning by *Amanita phalloides* as the means of seeing off the victim, and when he describes the circumstances and symptoms of the poisoning he knew exactly what he was talking about.

Todd's fascination with taxonomy was just one manifestation of a mind which constantly strived to bottom out every area of knowledge it encountered. Another example is his immersion in the technical details of how William Blake produced his prints – an area in which he became an acknowledged expert: the 'father' of William Blake studies, Sir Geoffrey Keynes, used to refer to Todd as 'The Mole' in recognition of his ability to ferret out obscure facts. In this, Todd was assisted by a type of photographic memory whereby he could remember for a long time in which book, and almost on which page, he had encountered a reference. There was an element of the obsessive in his need to pursue every area of enquiry to exhaustion, and it did at times become counterproductive in terms of the practical requirements of making a living as a writer.

Making money from nature

When Todd left Britain for America early in 1947 (soon after he had written the Stubbs novels) he began to write, and submit to publishers and magazines, various poems, articles and ideas for books which dealt with themes from nature. This he continued to do in fits and starts until his death in Mallorca in 1978. Some of these found their way into print, usually bringing only small financial reward, while many others lie in draft form gathering dust in university archives. The books he made most money out of were written for children, such as *The Tropical Fish Book* – an illustrated manual of how to set up and populate a tropical fish tank, and *Tan's Fish* – a delightful account (based on fact) of how a young Chinese boy discovers a new variety of fish, which is named after him. The story was ahead of its time in carrying a strong message relating to the conservation of endangered species. His biggest money-spinner during the Fifties, however, was his series of four children's books about a feline astronaut called Space Cat. These books combined and exploited two themes which were in vogue among American children at the time: cats and science fiction. In one of them, *Space Cat Meets Mars*, our hero lands on Mars – a Mars where mushrooms thrive in profusion (Figure 2). Other works never made it to publication, such as an educational book for children to be called *Molds and Mushrooms*, and an article on hallucinogenic plants and fungi.

During his lifetime Ruthven Todd was probably best known as a poet. Some have referred to him as a 'nature poet', including W. H. Auden, who wrote in 1961:

> As a 'nature poet', he is almost the only one today who is a real naturalist
> and can tell one bird or flower from another – his erudition in these matters
> makes me very jealous.[2]

but this labelling does not do justice to the breadth of his poetic output. In Britain, before and during World War Two, he wrote his share of anti-war poetry (he was a conscientious objector) and also wrote love poems (he was a serial faller-in-love) as well as poems of homage to poets and artists he

2   Dust-jacket of Todd, R. (1961) *Garland for the Winter Solstice*. London: Dent.

Figure 2. Front cover of *Space Cat Meets Mars*.

admired and ones in memory of lost friends. But it is true that many other poems did draw on themes from nature – at the end of this chapter is reproduced 'Of Moulds and Mushrooms', one he wrote in 1955 while living in Martha's Vineyard.

However, a more tangible legacy of Todd's fascination with flowers and fungi were the exquisitely detailed coloured drawings which he executed. Although in his own estimation Todd had no flair for creative art, there is no doubt that he was a first-rate technical illustrator: as a youth he spent school holidays working in the office of his father's architectural practice, and after leaving school he spent a year at Edinburgh College of Art. The illustrations of wild flowers and fungi which he created in America and later in Mallorca took the form both of illustrated diaries, where the illustrations surround his neat calligraphic handwriting (a page from one of his diaries is reproduced as a frontispiece to this book) and stand-alone drawings in pencil and water-colour. Some of these drawings he exhibited for sale in local venues, while others were done to commission, usually at prices which hardly reflected the effort required to produce them. Many he gave away to family and friends, where they have become treasured possessions. Those he did manage to sell supplemented a very uncertain income from writing, and helped him to keep his head above water financially, although he was at times reduced to a state of near poverty. After he had left Martha's Vineyard for Mallorca, friends tried to find a publisher for his journals illustrating the flora of the Vineyard, but none was found, primarily because of the expense and difficulty of doing justice to Todd's artwork.

Magic mushrooms

One of the more exotic byways of fungus lore deals with what is sometimes referred to as ethnomycology – the study of the use of mushrooms in ritual, religion and medicine. So-called 'mushroom rituals' typically involve the preparation and consumption of pyscho-active (hallucinogenic) mushrooms

such as the fly agarics and the psilocybes ('magic mushrooms'). There
is evidence that these mushrooms have been used in ritual contexts for
thousands of years in Europe and Mesoamerica, and the practice has
survived among small indigenous groups in Mexico and Guatemala until
recent times. The phenomenon was brought to the awareness of the public
in 1955, when a rich American banker and amateur mycologist (Robert)
Gordon Wasson participated in an ancient mushroom ritual which was still
being practised by a group of Mazatec people in the south Mexican province
of Oaxaca. He recorded the progress of the ritual and his experience of im-
bibing the juice of psilocybe mushrooms, later publishing an article about it
in *Life* magazine. Wasson and Todd had a common acquaintance in the poet
Robert Graves, whom Wasson had consulted about historical and mytho-
logical aspects of mushroom cults, and Wasson and Todd soon began to
correspond. Wasson recognised Todd's skill as an illustrator of mushrooms
and wanted to secure his services to illustrate a book he planned to pub-
lish. Todd, for his part, wanted Wasson to bring him back some psilocybe
mushrooms from Mexico. Todd enjoyed experimenting with psycho-active
compounds derived from plants, and wanted to compare the experience
of taking mescalin derived from the peyote cactus with the effect of taking psilocybe mushrooms. This interest seems to have been partly in the
genuine spirit of enquiry as fodder for an article he was writing, but he also
wrote to a friend that 'I would like to get mescalin more legally ... good to
have on hand when the imagination dims and life is at a low ebb.' Wasson
obliged by supplying him with some mushrooms, and Todd recorded that
he found the effect of the extract from them barely distinguishable from
mescalin, except that his hallucinogenic experience was overlaid with a
Mexican flavour – a type of auto-suggestion very similar to that reported by
Albert Hoffman (discoverer of LSD-25) when he first consumed psilocybe
mushrooms in 1943, knowing them to have been sourced from Mexico.

Mushroom stones

For a long time Mayan archaeologists had been recovering pre-Columbian
stone artefacts in the form of mushroom statues, typically a couple of feet
high, and often incorporating human or animal effigies on their stalks (see
Figure 4). The statues were assumed to have been associated with the
mushroom rituals, possibly acting as a type of pestle on which to prepare
the mushrooms for consumption. Mainly they were found in Guatemala,
although a few examples had been found from the south of Mexico. In the
early 1950s, Todd approached a friend of his whose services he used as a lit-

erary agent, but who also conducted amateur 'excavations' in Mexico and sold artefacts he found in a shop in Boston. Todd charged him with finding a mushroom stone to add to his own collection of curios. After some years of wrangling over arrangements to have the heavy artefact exported to Mallorca, it eventually arrived at Todd's home in the mountain village of Galilea at some time in the late 1960s. His mushroom stone was identified by Dr Stephan F. de Borhegyi (the 'last word' on the subject) as dating from 800 to 900 AD, and as originating

Figure 3. Todd's Mexican mushroom statue.

from Mexico. It had cost Todd some $50 in total, but he was told that it had a resale value of some hundreds of dollars. He was not tempted to sell, and it continued to adorn a dresser in Galilea until his death in 1978 (Figure 3).

As part of a project to mimic the printing techniques of William Blake in 1971, Todd designed a coloured print based on photographs from Gordon Wasson, which showed some ritual mushroom stones together with hallucinogenic mushrooms (Figure 4).

Marijuana

Todd's interest in hallucinogenic mushrooms extended into other drugs derived from plants, and at one stage when living in Mallorca he started to compile an encyclopaedia of such plants. As had other writers before him, he went to Mallorca in 1960 in part to join the literary court around Robert Graves, who had set up a home in the tiny mountain village of Deya. During the 1960s, Mallorca, and Deya in particular, became infested with young drug-taking hippies from abroad. In 1966, a Californian 'drug guru' David Solomon arrived with his family and became a prime mover amongst its drug-taking community. Both Graves and Todd were in danger of being sucked into his slipstream through their interest in narcotic and hallucinogenic plants. Throughout his life Todd had been well-known among his friends for his inability to distinguish desirable from undesirable associates, and for a period he became friendly with Solomon, who supplied him with

Figure 4. Todd's print showing mushroom stones and hallucinogenic mushrooms.

charas, a form of cannabis resin manufactured in the Indian subcontinent. This he consumed, with some rather undramatic consequences which he recorded in an unpublished diary of 1966. The Franco regime took a predictably dim view of drug-peddling, and Solomon quickly found himself in prison. An appeal to Todd to speak on his behalf in court was wisely refused, and Todd thus extricated himself from a potentially dangerous situation. (Ironically, the trial judges visited Todd to borrow books about marijuana from his library.) Solomon escaped conviction but was kicked out of Spain, after which he moved to Britain, became involved with a gang manufacturing LSD, and was sentenced to ten years' imprisonment.

Todd's attitude to drug-taking in general was, as one might expect, at the liberal end of the spectrum. He himself consumed tobacco and alcohol to excess. Like David Solomon, he believed that cannabis should be legalised, although he stated himself to be opposed to the legalisation of opium derivatives and cocaine, because of the social damage they inflicted. He had no moral scruples about the use of hallucinogenic drugs, although he personally shunned LSD because he believed it to be dangerously strong and because, as an ergot derivative, it carried a risk of developing gangrene.

Milk of Paradise

In 1966, an idle question posed by Richard Hull, a friend of Todd's who was engaged in translating the works of Carl Jung into English, set Todd off on a new journey of mole-like research. He asked Todd, as a naturalist, whether he thought it possible that the German word *waldhonig* (literally, 'forest honey') was the same as the English 'honeydew'. *Waldhonig* is mentioned by Jung as a substance known to the sixteenth century Swiss alchemist Paracelsus for its ability to induce a state of exaltation. This set Todd to thinking about whether there was a connection with the use of 'honeydew' by Coleridge in his drug-induced poetry fragment *Kubla Khan*, where it is used in the final lines:

> For he on honey-dew hath fed,
> And drunk the milk of Paradise.

Honeydew is a sweet, sticky substance excreted by aphids and deposited on the leaves and stems of certain plants and trees, but the word is also used to describe the excrescence of the fungus *Claviceps purpurea*, better known as ergot, a substance from which Albert Hoffman first synthesised LSD-25 in 1943. The fungus, for which rye grass is a common host, has led to historic outbreaks of ergotism – a disease characterised by convulsions and gangrene, and once known as St Anthony's Fire. Such an outbreak occurred in France in 1951,[3] where the cause was the consumption of tainted rye bread. After a year of intensive correspondence with experts on Coleridge, Paracelsus and fungi, Todd published an article in *London Magazine* in March 1967 entitled 'Coleridge and Paracelsus; Honeydew and LSD'. It is quite a well-argued piece which comprises only about four pages of text, but seven pages of notes and references. Put simply, its thesis was that both Coleridge and Paracelsus were referring to the same substance, and that they were well aware of its hallucinogenic properties.

Todd planned to follow up this publication with a further three articles (or even a book) taking his ideas further. One of these ideas concerned Xenophon's account in *Anabasis* of how in 401 BC ten thousand Greek soldiers retreating from Persia were poisoned by eating honey which they found at Trebizond. Todd believed that they were actually poisoned by ergot which is known to favour wild grasses common in the Trebizond region as a host: 'I am convinced that the ten thousand at Trebizond were all as high as kites

---

3   In the 1960s, the circumstances of this outbreak were revisited as the plot for an episode of the television series *Dr Finlay's Casebook*, entitled *Coming Through the Rye*.

on ergot'. However, the *London Magazine* article never generated the level of interest he hoped for, and the later articles remain as unpublished fragments. The article certainly generated no income – quite the reverse. He received £25 for it, but researching it had cost him far more for postage and xerox copying.

Mushroom lover

Ruthven Todd's lifelong interest in fungi never made him much money, but he derived intellectual stimulus from researching and writing about them. He was a good cook, and loved eating wild mushrooms. He was among the last of the great fungus illustrators, before colour photography took over. Towards the end of his life, even after his eyesight was failing, he laboriously coloured, by hand, writing paper pre-printed with his mushroom drawings, to write to his friends. In the draft of an article to be called *A Bit about Mushrooms*, but which was never published, he reflected on his own feelings about them:

> In my time, I have written poems about mushrooms and I have made pictures of them. Now I sit and recall them all, and still have pleasure in the thought of the spongy underneaths of *cèpes*, the curious roughness of the turtle-shelled puffballs, the leathery surface of the beefsteak, the fragile Venetian blinds of the agarics, the rumpled sides of the horns of plenty. Of such textures can a life be made, and lived with pure delight.[4]

The Death Cap is the only example of Todd's fiction where mushrooms are central to the story, and where he transplanted his own expertise so directly to a fictional character - the remarkable Professor John Stubbs.

---

4   Todd, R. (n.d.) *A Bit About Mushrooms* (unpublished typescript). MS26861. Edinburgh: National Library of Scotland.

Of Moulds and Mushrooms

Agrippina, well aware of Claudius' greed
For Caesar's mushroom, knew also that it looked
Like death-cap or destroying angel, so a god
Made room on earth for Nero, whose joke,
'Food of the gods,' allowed for deadly poison.

Some still, with unreasoning fear, disgust,
Kick or switch down the mushrooms by their path,
Leaving the amanita rudely shattered, gills
Like fallen feathers scattered, veil and volva
Broken, and all this symmetry destroyed.

The lack of chlorophyll suggests the parasite
Which guilty man so readily despises.
These are strange fruit of the thin mycelium,
That webs this world beneath the surface,
And which can persist in its invisibility

Breaking down discard of leaves and timber,
Which otherwise would overtop the wood
Extinguishing everything, so that the seed
May sprout to nourishment, and the cycle
Of death, decay and rebirth still go on.

And I, aesthetic and somewhat botanical,
Would note and praise the diversity
Of shapes, variety and colours of the fungi,
Ball, club, shelf, parasol, cup and horn,
And the suave velvet of the different moulds.

I would recall the fungi in their settings:
Fly-agaric, scarlet with wrinkled creamy warts,
In birch woods of Dumbartonshire, but lemon-
Yellow in New England, toxic they said to flies,
But intoxicant for the Kamchatka tribesman.

Near Selkirk once I found a monstrous puffball,
Far bigger than my younger brother's head,
A gleaming baldpate beckoning me across the field
To find and greet poor Yorick's vegetable skull,
Solitary underneath the well-clipped hazel hedge.

Where anciently the monks had had their abbey,
Beside my Essex farmhouse, clustered blewits
Were palely violet below the dark-fruited sloes,

THE DEATH CAP

And the old gnarled oaks within the woods
Were sometimes richly shelved with beefsteaks;

And I, in a strictly rationed world,
Welcomed and ate these, and others that I found,
Spongy cèpe, chantrelle and honeycombed morel,
Grey oyster-mushroom and tall dignified parasol,
Which I again met later on a Chilmark lawn.

Brown-purple trumpets of the cornucopia
Stand clear against the brilliance of the moss
Under a clump of beech-trees at Gay Head,
While vast fairy-rings, some centuries of age,
Manacle the cropped grass of the South Downs.

The wooden ships of England knew dry-rot,
Pepys gathering toadstools bigger than his fists,
So that ten oaks were cut for each one used,
And the white-rimmed tawniness rioted again
Among the bombed buildings that I sometime knew.

Fungi have made their share of history:
St Anthony's fire, from ergot in the rye,
Swept savagely through medieval France,
Rotting potatoes drove the Irishman abroad,
And French grapes grow on North American stock.

A mouldering cantaloupe from a Peoria supermarket
Supplanted the culture Fleming kept for years,
And others now sample soil, remove and scan
The moulds that, in their destructiveness,
Aid ailing man by driving out his enemies.

But I, walking in fields or through the woods,
Welcome the vermilion russula, the sulphur
Polyporus, or inky shaggy-cap upon a heap of dung,
Without questioning their usefulness to me.
The ecology of my appreciation seems to need

Clavaria's coral branches on a damp dark bank,
Odorous stink-horns prodding through the grass,
And petalled dry geasters studding by a sandy road.
These many-fangled fruits make bright
My sundry places where no flowers can bloom.

Ruthven Todd, Martha's Vineyard, 1955.

The Death Cap

CHAPTER ONE

CAP AND BELLS[5]

LIKE THE history of the House of Stuart this story begins with a girl.[6] A honey, a peach, a winner, or whatever else you like to call her. Her name was Mary Winstone and I met her at a party. I'm always meeting people at parties, but mostly they drop out of my life as if they never had existed. Mostly, too, I'm not sorry to see them go.

As a rule one can divide the people one meets at parties into several distinct classes or species. There's the chap who, under the benevolent influence of alcohol, appears to be the fellow you've been hoping to meet for years – as sympathetic as a sponge – and usually as absorbent. Then there's the fellow who bores you from the start; you just don't seem able to find a piece of ground where you both can stand, and finally there are the people whom you meet at every party you go to. You never see them apart from parties and so far as you know they hibernate during the dry seasons.

Mary was none of these. As soon as I saw her through the fug of small talk and cigarette smoke I knew that. Tall and black haired, with an oval face, I wanted to meet her as soon as I could. I pushed my way rudely through the clusters of people who were talking about everything from the ballet to the water colours of Paul Klee.

I never was much good at dissembling. Like the old man, Professor John Stubbs, I believe in going for my fences and not in looking round in the hope that there may be a gate half a mile down the field.

"Hullo," I said cheerfully, as that seemed as good a greeting as any other, "have a cigarette?"

5 The title of a poem by William Butler Yeats.
6 Presumably a reference to Mary Queen of Scots who is believed to have changed the spelling from *Stewart* to *Stuart* to make the name more pronounceable for the French.

She expressed her willingness to have a cigarette, and everything would have been fine if I'd been able to find my packet of Player's.[7] I dug through my pockets and encountered a great deal that had no right to be there, but I was damned if I could find a fag. I had to bum one off a chap who was passing, a tall thin fellow with a sad face. His name was Douglas Newsome and he wrote poems. Some of them were good and he knew I thought they were, so he surrendered his cigarettes without a murmur.

The only trouble then was that having scrounged Newsome's cigarettes I had to think of some way of getting rid of him. He seemed to know the girl already and gave me a sort of introduction but he would hang around. Finally his tonsils became a trifle dry and he wandered off sadly in search of a drink. He was the sort of young man who never looked cheerful. If it wasn't political troubles in the Far East,[8] he was sure to have a pain in his stomach.

"My name's Boyle," I said, adding to the low mumble, which Newsome had used something in the way of clarity, "Max Boyle. What's yours? I didn't get it all from Douglas."

She told me and her voice was just what I'd have expected. It was the sort of voice which gets me every time. Deep but not too deep, and gentle without being soporific.

After that we got on fine. I discovered that she was an actress. She worked at a repertory theatre in a small town in Essex, but was not taking part in the current production and so had been able to get up to town for a day or two, by way of a holiday.

Until I met her the party had seemed like nearly all other parties I had been to. Full of people who would insist on lecturing me upon subjects in which I had no interest whatsoever. Among these subjects I had hitherto included theatrical shop. So far as I was concerned I went to the theatre to see a play and I came away having seen it. I was not interested in the mechanics which made it go. I did not wish to know about the squabbles which took place behind the scenes.

Now it seemed that I wanted to hear nothing else. I could have sat for

7   John Player & Sons, a Nottingham-based company which eventually became part of the Imperial Tobacco Group, was the first to market pre-packaged tobacco. Player's Navy Cut cigarettes, with the distinctive sailor logo on the packet, can still be bought today.

8   Perhaps a reference to the constitutional reform being undertaken in post-war Japan.

hours listening to Mary's voice telling me about Bobbie and Phil and Jackie and Alec. I had no idea of the sex of these mysterious and disembodied Christian names and when I guessed I usually guessed the wrong way. Also these Christian names seemed to have little to do with the names which their possessors presented to the public. It was all very muddling.

I think I should go back a bit now, leaving myself talking to Mary, and say something about myself, the me that's telling this story.

I've already said that my name's Max Boyle and that I work for Professor Stubbs, botanist and detective – the great panjandrum[9] himself with the little round button on top and the gunpowder running out of the heels of his boots.

After we had cleared up the mess of the bodies in the bookshop,[10] I thought I was really due to take my holiday, but not a bit of it. The old man never takes a holiday himself and he seems to think I'm built of the same heroic stuff.

When we got home he dismissed the case from his mind and sat down to work on his overdue *History of Botany*, a book that has about as much chance of appearing this side of the year two thousand as I have of living to that date.

"Oi," I said when I saw what he was up to, "you'd better leave that till I get back from my holiday."

"Holiday?" his broad face was as innocent as that of an owlet, "You're not goin' for a holiday are you?"

"Oh, no," my voice was as caustic as I could make it, "I don't really need a holiday. I can just work myself to a frazzle month in and month out – I don't need a holiday."

I should have known better than to try sarcasm on the old man. He paid no attention to my tone of voice but only to the sense of my words. He sighed with relief and let his steel-rimmed glasses slide down to the end of his blunt nose.

9 As well as being the title of a poem written by Samuel Foote (1720-1777) to test the memory of the actor Charles Macklin, the great panjandrum was the name given to an experimental weapon designed to destroy the concrete defences that the Germans had built on the French coast in the Second World War. It consisted of two large rocket-propelled wheels between which was a large drum of explosives.

10 See *Bodies in a Bookshop*, published by John Westhouse in 1946 and reprinted by Dover in 1984.

"I knew ye were only jokin'. Ye wouldn't do a thin' like that to me, would ye now, Max?"

There was no help for it. I gave up my idea of a nice holiday by the sea-side and settled down to work. I might have gone on arguing with the Professor till I got my own way, but then I'd just have been laying up a penance for myself. It was quite clear that he had determined to go ahead with his work on the damned *History* and he'd have done it whether I was with him or in Timbuctoo.[11]

When the old man works like that I know what happens. He covers the whole of the floor with scraps of paper covered with notes in his neat handwriting, and if I'm not there to pick them up and file them they get more and more involved and entangled, and what is worse, some of them are apt to get lost. And that isn't all. I've more or less perfected the most involved filing system in the world. I know where to find any reference the Professor wants at the very shortest notice. The fly in that ointment is the old man himself. He has about as much idea of a filing system as a belted tapir[12] has. He wants a reference and he wants it in a hurry, so he starts on the files with the air of a most determined anteater attacking an anthill. After he's done this once or twice the system ceases to be a system. That's all.

I resigned myself to the idea of staying at home until the old man thought of something he wanted to do which would not involve me in quite so much work after my holiday.

At the same time I was justifiably and understandingly hopping mad. I would not work more than a certain number of hours a day. After the tenth hour had finished I would finish too. I was downright about that fact, and to make certain the old man worked up no purgatory for me in the morning I locked the steel filing-cabinet and put the key in my pocket. That ditched him good and proper. He had to fill in the evenings working on something else.

The older I grow the more convinced I become that there should be some sort of trade union to look after the interests of those who are unfortunate enough to work for scientists of the calibre of John Stubbs. I don't

11 Timbuctoo is an African city which, by the fifteenth century, was a centre for Islamic study and home to a university and an extensive library of manuscripts, sadly threatened by modern-day conflicts.

12 This is probably a reference to the Malayan tapir which has a distinctive white band across its back and sides.

believe that man *needs* sleep at all – he only does it sometimes because he was brought up to and what was good enough for his parents is good enough for him.

Anyhow, I took to going out in the evenings. Once or twice I went out with the old man but I was damned wary on these occasions, as I remembered what had happened when I took him to a bottle-party.[13] Some people get burrs when they go walking in a country lane – well, that's the way the old man gets murders. If he goes to tea with his maiden aunt, her maid chooses to run amok and murder the vicar in the front garden just as the Professor is sipping his tea. It seems to me that people wait till he's around before deciding to do their killing.

It is almost as if they said, "Oh, good, here comes the old man. Let's think up a juicy murder and do it, now, to see how puzzled he gets." So, smack, they bump someone off and sit back and wait to be arrested. I get no pleasure out of murders. I've got no hunting instinct. Give me a few plants and a job of work to do on them – working out chromosome patterns or whatnot – and I'm happy.

Among the places which I took to haunting during my evenings out were two pubs – one of them in St. Martin's Lane,[14] called *The Salisbury*,[15] and the other, in Charlotte Street,[16] called *The Fitzroy*.[17]

These places gave me a kick of an odd sort. They were full of the never do any work and never shalls. Those who were going to paint *the* great picture of the century or write *the* great novel – but never to-day or tomorrow, always the day after. The habitués were dreamers on the grand scale to whom alcohol had become more than a stimulant, or even a necessity

13 See *Take Thee a Sharp Knife*, published by John Westhouse in 1946, and reprinted by Lomax Press in 2012.

14 St. Martin's Lane runs south from the junction of Garrick Street and Cranbourn Street to the church of St. Martin-in-the-Fields, after which it is named.

15 *The Salisbury* was built in 1899 by the founder of the London Brick Company, John Cathles Hill, on a site leased from the Marquis of Salisbury. It is a Grade II* listed building (i.e. one of particular importance) in the French Renaissance style.

16 Charlotte Street was built in 1763 and is named after Queen Charlotte, the wife of King George III.

17 *The Fitzroy Tavern* is located at 16 Charlotte Street and was a popular meeting place for writers, artists and intellectuals in the inter-war and immediately post-war years. It was popularly known as Kleinfeld's after the owner Judah Kleinfeld.

in the dipsomaniac manner. After a certain number of drinks they knew exactly what the picture was going to took like; they could describe the frame and the colour scheme and sometimes even the composition. Or they knew how their book was to be bound, on what hand-made paper the limited edition was to be printed, and even how it would be received by the periodical reviewers. Ralph Straus,[18] with his usual kindly word for everyone, would be unusually kind. Desmond McCarthy[19] would make the book the subject of his column in *The Sunday Times*,[20] and Charles Morgan[21] would reflect it in Menander's Mirror[22] in *The Times Literary Supplement*.[23] Even Geoffrey Grigson[24] would admire it, and Cyril Connolly[25] would suggest an article in *Horizon*.[26]

But, between the dream and the actuality there came the awful job of really settling down to work. The strain of putting brush to canvas or pen to paper upset the flow of the imagination. I am not sneering at those people when I say this, for I believe it to be an absolutely true fact that there was some trauma between their imaginations and their creative abilities.

18 Ralph Straus (1882-1950) was a reviewer for *The Sunday Times* and *The Bystander*. He was also a book collector and author of fiction and non-fiction, including several works on the history of printing.

19 Desmond McCarthy (1877-1952) was a reviewer and literary journalist for *The Sunday Times*. He had previously been literary editor of *The New Statesman*, reviewing books under the pen-name of Affable Hawk.

20 At the time of the story *The Sunday Times* was part of the Kemsley Newspaper Group and employed Ian Fleming as its foreign editor.

21 Charles Langridge Morgan (1894-1958) was a novelist who also wrote for *The Times, The New York Times* and *The Times Literary Supplement*.

22 Menander was an ancient Greek dramatist who wrote more than a hundred comedies. The name may have been chosen by Morgan because he was a drama critic early in his career and also wrote three plays.

23 Most of the reviews that appeared in *The Times Literary Supplement* appeared anonymously until 1974.

24 Geoffrey Grigson (1905-1985) was a poet, writer, critic and naturalist, and an important influence on Todd. He was, as Cerberus, the editor of *New Verse* for which Todd wrote a number of poems.

25 Cyril Connolly (1903-1974) was a literary critic and writer who founded and edited the magazine *Horizon: A Review of Literature and Art* from 1940-1949.

26 *Horizon: A Review of Literature and Art* was a relatively short-lived, but highly influential, magazine founded by Cyril Connolly and Peter Watson. Todd worked as an editor for *Horizon* at the start of the war, and also contributed a number of articles and poems, including an article on Paul Klee.

At any rate, I like them, in small doses, and some of them actually did manage to work. Roger Sharon, for instance. He was not a good painter – in fact he was a damned bad one – but I will say for him that he knew what painting was about. He taught me to appreciate the works of Paul Klee and told me things about the art of painting which made me begin to understand Picasso.

Like all the others, Roger had his dream of the picture he was going to paint, but he knew more about it than the others did. He had some money of his own and rented a small house in Mecklenburgh Square.[27]

This house had a good many rooms and in each of them Roger had put a divan bed and many other odds and ends he had managed to pick up. The result was that his house had become a sort of superior Rowton House.[28] Anyone who liked could stay there, and stay as long as they liked so long as they did not disturb Roger, who liked to lie late in the mornings, nursing whatever he had gathered in the way of a hangover the previous evening.

It was his party I was attending. The sort of party where the host lays in a few gallons of beer and perhaps brews a punch, but relies upon his guests to bring the rest of the drink. Most people seemed to have raised a drink or two.

When I had told the old man I was going to a party he had almost begged me to let him accompany me. I was still feeling pretty sick with him about the loss of my holiday and, in addition, he hadn't been invited, so I left him at home, churning away at a paper for the *Journal of Genetics*.[29]

"Look here," I'd said as I left, "I promise you that I'll take you to the next party I'm invited to, but I can't take you to this one. You know that your presence is inclined to cramp my style?"

"Cramp yer style, boy," he had roared at me, rising like a trout to a

---

27 Todd lived at number 18 Mecklenburgh Square which he rented in 1943 from the Foundling Hospital Trust until the property was bombed in 1944.

28 The Rowton Houses, also mentioned in Orwell's *Down and Out in Paris and London*, were working men's hostels funded by the Victorian philanthropist Lord Rowton (1838-1903). There were six Rowton Houses in London at the time of the story.

29 The *Journal of Genetics* is one of the oldest journals in its field and was founded in 1910 by William Bateson (1861-1926) and Reginald Crundall Punnett (1875-1967).

Greenwell's Glory,[30] "ye know I can't do that. Ye leave me for a moment an' ye go tumblin' head over heels into trouble. All right, I'll take ye up on yer promise."

What the old man said about trouble was my own opinion about him. If I leave him alone for a couple of days I always feel afraid that he's pinched the Crown Jewels in my absence – just to show that it could be done. All the same I was glad that I had not brought the Professor with me. He is a much bigger man than I am, in all ways, and he might have stolen the little bit of thunder I was rolling out for myself.

"Where are you staying while you are in town, Mary?" I asked. One good thing that must be said for theatrical people is that they do not cling on to the formality of the surname for a second longer than is necessary. "Are you living in a hotel?"

"Why?" she asked, without surprise, but obviously just for the sake of making conversation. I did not feel that I was progressing very fast, so I tried again.

"Oh," my voice was light with an airiness I did not feel, "I was just wondering whether you would eat something with me once this party comes to an end and whether I could see you home?"

She looked around the room. As she moved her head the heavy black hair swung round her white neck.

"Oh," she said, "I'm staying here. Roger offered to put me up, and I don't think I really want to go out to-night. We'll probably rig up an omelette or something after the party finishes. Though it doesn't seem to be showing any signs of finishing, does it?"

I glanced around. The party still seemed to be going strong. The pale yellow rush matting on the floor was dotted with cigarette-ends and there were one or two dark patches where people had upset glasses of beer. In the far corner, beside a table which was doing duty as a bar, Roger was engaged in putting a record on the gramophone.

The tumpity of Fats Waller[31] playing the piano cut through the drone of conversation and his deep voice announced that his very good friend the

30 Greenwells' Glory is a fishing fly devised by Canon William Greenwell (1820-1918) of Durham, in 1854. The first, and highly popular, variation was devised by E.M. Tod in 1903.

31 Fats Waller (1904-1943) was a jazz pianist and singer whose successful career was cut short when he contracted a fatal bout of pneumonia.

milkman told him he was missing his sleep.[32]

A little fat man came up and stood beside us. Mary looked up at him.

"Oh, Alec darling," she said, with the meaningless endearment of the actress, "this is Max Boyle."

I unwound my rather long length from the edge of the chair where I had placed it. The little man gave me a little damp paw. I relinquished it as soon as it appeared to be decent to do so. He took the other arm of the chair and sat down.

"Stella seems to be enjoying herself," he announced portentously. I followed his glance and saw a little red haired girl who was clinging on to a big man with a face that looked as though it had known better days before it had been run over by a steam-roller.

"Oh you know, Alec," Mary replied, "she's got a terrific thing about Harold. I'm sure she dreams of him all the time."

"I can't see what she sees in him myself," Alec, whose last name it transpired was Dolittle, replied. "She seems to think that he's a god. I suppose it must be the primitive appeal of the brute or something of the sort, eh?"

I didn't seem to be much in on this conversation, but I knew who the big man was. He was an ex-all-in-wrestler called Harold Ironside – I don't believe that was his real name – it sounded too good to be true. Having left the doubtful pleasures of the mat, Ironside had made up his mind that he would be a sculptor. The odd thing was that he sculpted things so far removed from himself – gazelles and pigeons and ballet dancers. He was one of the people who had moved into Roger's house and had dug himself into a niche.

The party seemed to be gradually folding itself up. A few people left the room and the cigarette smoke swirled out with them, leaving the air rather clearer. I looked round the walls at the pictures which Roger had gathered. He had the good sense and the good taste to leave his own pictures off his walls. There was a nice gouache by the Catalan artist, Joan Miró,[33] and a good drawing by Henry Moore[34] of some red shapes standing up before a wall as if waiting to be shot. Behind the gramophone there hung Picasso's

32 The lyrics to *My Very Good Friend the Milkman* were written by Johnny Burke, and the song was first recorded by Fats Waller in 1935.

33 Todd was a friend of Miró and owned one of his gouaches.

34 Todd was also a friend of Moore and owned one of his sculptures.

large etching of the Minotaur[35] flanked on each side by his aquatints called *The Dream and Lies of Franco*.[36] Opposite me there hung a small water colour by Klee and his lithograph of the little man walking a tight rope[37] was also on the walls.

The conversation between Alec Dolittle and Mary seemed to be rather concerned with things which I knew nothing about. The names of people of whom I had never heard drifted through it like butterflies, to be pinned with the bright phrase.

I got up and excused myself. I wandered down the room to pour myself a drink. All this wit which was being expended made me feel rather thirsty.

Roger was a bit tight. In fact I think he was probably rather tighter than anyone in the room, with the exception of Douglas Newsome who had gone to sleep on a sofa with his mouth open. But then I had nothing against a chap getting tight at his own party – so far as I'm concerned I think there's nothing like it as you don't need to bother about getting home afterwards.

"Hullo, Roger," I said rather inanely, "damned good party isn't it?"

"I'm glad you think so," he replied, rather petulantly, "because I, myself, think it stinks. I think nearly everybody here stinks too, if you want to know."

I didn't want to know, but I wondered why he was so depressed. It wasn't like him to feel that way. Most times I had met Roger he had seemed to be so full of the milk of human kindness that you could have offered him to the United Dairies.[38] He was one of the people who really did seem to like other people – just as people without bothering about them as individuals.

"What's the matter?" I asked, dipping the neck of a bottle of whisky into a glass. "It seems to be a pretty nice party full of pretty nice people."

I was feeling pretty good. Partly my goodness may have been due to the drink, but mostly I think it was due to the fact that I'd met with Mary. I am a pretty susceptible person and I knew I was falling. I know all the symptoms.

---

35 Possibly *The Minotaur*, produced in the 1930s.

36 Todd is believed to have owned a print of this picture.

37 *Tightrope Walker* was produced by Klee in 1923.

38 United Dairies was formed in 1917 from the merger of three dairy companies, and by 1950 had expanded, through numerous acquistions, to be the largest company in its sector. It is now part of Unigate.

"Oh, I don't know," Roger brushed his depression aside, "I suppose I may have upset my liver or something."

He turned round to the gramophone and put on a record of Jimmy Yancey.[39] As he straightened up after changing the needle I saw that his glance was fixed on Harold Ironside. As they say, if looks could kill, Harold would have been mouldering in his grave.

I took my drink neat, wondering what all the trouble was about.

[39] Jimmy Yancey (1894-1951) was a boogie-woogie pianist who famously ended every piece in E flat.

CHAPTER TWO

THE WEIGHT OF CHANCE DESIRES[40]

WHEN I woke in the morning I felt pretty good. I should have had a head ringing with all the bells in Bow,[41] but my eye was clear and my liver untroubled.

I had given up trying to cheer Roger and had drifted back to Mary. Alec Dolittle was still there, cracking epigrams at the expense of his friends, but after a few minutes he realised his glass was empty and took it and Mary's to get a refill. I took the opportunity and made a date with Mary to have dinner with me the next evening.

It was clear to me that Mary did not positively dislike me and the thought was pleasant. As I shaved I more or less said to the stubble, "She loves me, she loves me not, she loves me, she loves me not." I was as callow as a schoolboy, but then, I told myself, it wasn't every day that you met a girl like Mary.

I pushed my way through the piles of books which had gathered in my room by some mysterious agency, and wandered down the stairs, whistling to myself. As I did my nursemaid act with the plants that had settled in the Professor's room like ragwort on a bombed site, my whistle became louder.

"Hell, Max," a loud voice said rudely, "if ye can't whistle in tune, don't whistle at all."

I turned round and there was the old man. He was wrapped to the neck in an immense tartan dressing-gown of uncertain age. My private opinion

40 Wordsworth's *Ode to Duty* contains the lines: "Me this uncharter'd freedom tires; I feel the weight of chance desires".

41 The bells of St-Mary-le-Bow have long been associated with London life and tradition. The original bells were destroyed in the Great Fire of London (1666) and were recast and augmented a number of times. By the time of the story they had been destroyed again, this time by the Luftwaffe in an air raid of 1941.

is that it belonged to Rob Roy MacGregor[42] and was responsible for the edict against wearing tartan.[43]

Although he had not yet breakfasted, the Professor had his filthy little pipe stuck in his mouth distilling its vile and evil smoke. How he does it on an empty stomach beats me.

"What do you know about tune?" I demanded. "When you sing the crows come round you looking for their long lost brother."

As repartee it wasn't brilliant, but it was the best I could do on the spur of the moment.

The old man grinned round the stem of his pipe. He shook his head and his thick grey hair waved like a plume on a helmet.

"Same old Max, eh?" he growled, "I can always get a rise out o' ye. Did ye ha' a good party an' did ye get stinkin' drunk, as ye always do?"

This was a slander on my ability to hold my liquor. I let it pass. After all I haven't got the cubic capacity of the Professor. I can't put away thirty or forty pints of beer in a day. My legs are not at all hollow.

I told the Professor as much as I saw fit of my evening. In a way I felt sorry that I had not taken him with me, for he so obviously enjoyed talking about the party. On the other hand, remembering the look in Roger's eye as he glanced across the room and remembering the old man's habit of making murders spring up around him, I thought it was just as well that he hadn't come with me.

For all the good my reticence about Mary did me, I might just as well have announced my situation from the housetops. The old man peered at me over the steel rims of his glasses.

"Ye seem uncommon happy for the mornin' after," he observed, "an' ye seem uncommon cagey about yer own doin's o' the evenin'. What is it? A girl, eh? Ye fallin' in love again?"

"Again," I began hotly, but realised that the Professor was riding me, "I don't make a habit of falling in love. Do I now?"

42 Rob Roy (1671-1734) was a folk hero, outlaw or common criminal, depending on which side you favour in the Jacobite rebellions. The Crown finally exacted its revenge through the commissioning of a statue which stands near the Albert Hall in Stirling.

43 *The Dress Act* of 1746 banned the wearing of Highland dress, including tartan and the kilt, with a punishment of six months for the first offence, and transportation for seven years for a second one.

He grinned at me. A large chunk of toast covered with thick pieces of Cooper's Oxford marmalade[44] disappeared into the cavern of his mouth.

"Well," he mumbled, "if ye don't make a habit o' it, I don't know what ye'd call it. Seems to me ye're always fallin'. One o' these days ye'll hurt yerself."

"Um, yes," I said slowly, "I see your point. You go around in terror that I might get married and then you wouldn't have me available at all hours of the day and night. Isn't that it?"

"Touché," he growled at me. I will say that for the Professor. He is honest about things. He knows that I do my best to keep the papers and the books in some sort of order.

The morning's work went well. I undid the files and arranged all the notes which the old man had piled in a basket which we keep for the purpose. It is one of these immense yellow cane baskets[45] which come from the Canary Islands filled with new potatoes and it has the advantage over most wastepaper baskets in that even the Professor has not yet succeeded in making it overflow. I typed out the notes and put them away, adding them to my elaborate cross-index which enables me to find anything when I want it. This cross-index is a necessity as I found that if I filed anything under its principal heading only, the Professor was sure to want it for one of the lesser subjects.

I worked very well that day. I didn't want to give the old man any handle to beat me with when I announced that I wanted to knock off a bit early. I usually worked till eight o'clock, which meant that I'd done a pretty fair day slugging at it, but I wanted to knock off at five. I managed to reduce the pulp of notes to something resembling an ordered system and I started on the job of rearranging the books.

Sometimes it seems to me that I spend the whole of my life at the job of trying to keep the books on the shelves where they belong. The trouble is that both the old man and myself are inveterate book buyers. When we see something we want we buy it, whether we can afford it or not. We have learned our lesson that he who hesitates loses the book. As a result of this

44 Oxford marmalade is a very dark, bitter-sweet marmalade containing thick pieces of Seville orange peel. It was first created by Sarah Cooper in 1874 and became the main brand produced by the firm of Frank Cooper.

45 When helping Geoffrey Grigson to weed out submissions sent in for *New Verse* at Grigson's Hampstead house, Todd assigned them to one of three such baskets.

habit there is a continual flow of new books into the house, and nobody has yet invented elastic bookshelves. The old man just plants books on the tops of others or wherever he sees a space into which he can jam them. The consequence is that I find the latest detective stories hobnobbing with the earliest publications of the Royal Society[46] and books of verse peering bewilderedly out from the files of learned periodicals.

Once upon a time – the phrase gives a suggestion of my feelings – I had set to work and managed to get all the books into apple-pie order. Each author had his place on the shelves and every shelf in the house looked neat. I might just as well have saved my labour and given it to a worthy cause. The old man knows where to find things when everything is in a muddle, but give him an ordered system and he's flummoxed. I flummoxed him all right. Like the encroaching sand on the coast of Kent the mess came over us again. Books I had never seen in my life materialised suddenly in my bedroom.

Speaking as a scientist I must admit that I can find no reason to believe in poltergeists, but looking round my room I sometimes wonder. I really cannot blame Mrs. Farley, the Professor's housekeeper, for it all. Maybe she does occasionally dump something in my room, but I'm damned if I can see how she makes a copy of Boyle[47] (my illustrious namesake) on *The Spring and Weight of the Air*[48] suddenly pop up there. I require some logical explanation of the way a book, which I did not know we possessed, is suddenly made to appear among my things. When it is only a simple matter of a book or an object being transferred from one part of the house to another I can think of dozens of possible explanations, but some things beat me. I've seriously thought of putting the spiritualist people on to the job. Even the old man is sometimes fuddled by the way things materialise. Of course, he *may* have bought them a long time ago and forgotten them,

46 The Royal Society was founded in 1660 to promote knowledge of the natural world through observation and experiment. It is the oldest scientific academy in continuous existence in the world, and has a membership of over 1,400 of the world's greatest scientists.

47 Robert Boyle (1627-1691) was born into immense wealth and was thus able to dedicate himself to the pursuit of scientific knowledge. He was one of the founding members of the Royal Society and a significant chemist, physicist and inventor.

48 *The Spring and Weight of the Air* was first published in 1660 and in it Boyle described his experiments using a new vacuum pump that he had developed, and demonstrated the importance of the empirical approach in science.

when they might become silted over with his muddle and, in the course of years, suddenly work their way to the surface again.

I locked my filing cabinet in the face of the old man's wrath and strolled down the hill to catch a 24 bus,[49] which deposited me in the Charing Cross Road[50] in nice time to wander along to the *Arts Theatre Club*[51] in Great Newport Street,[52] where I had arranged to meet Mary.

Of course I was far too early. Whenever I have a date with a girl I am too early. It seems to be my fate to be the one who waits. Every now and again I make up my mind that I'll be late, just to see what happens. I've only done it once; I was half an hour late but the girl managed to be three-quarters of an hour. So I still had to wait. But I wasn't going to keep Mary waiting. I could feel it coming on me that I'd got it really badly.

When she turned up Mary looked slightly worried. I could see that. She apologised for being late and I drifted over to the bar and got a couple of drinks from Paddy, the barman.

"Cheerio," I said, putting the drink where it belonged, "what's up? You seem to be a bit worried. Are you feeling quite well?"

"Oh, *I'm* feeling grand," she replied, "but it's Stella. She's had the most frightful pains in her inside and has been most horribly sick all day."

"Has she seen a doctor?" I asked, rather unnecessarily, but it was the only thing to say.

"No," Mary frowned, "she won't see a doctor. She says she was brought up as a Christian Scientist[53] and has never seen a doctor in her life. She's

49 A contemporary *Hansard* (4th November 1946, vol 428, c174W) records that "London Passenger Transport Board have issued a reminder to their staff that passengers on omnibus route No. 24 to Hampstead may continue their journey to the terminus if they so wish."

50 Charing Cross Road has had a long association with second-hand, specialist and antiquarian booksellers, and runs north from St. Martin-in-the-Fields to Oxford Street. Todd worked for a period at Zwemmer's Bookshop in Charing Cross Road and said it was the first proper job he ever had.

51 The *Arts Theatre Club* was founded in 1927 as a members-only club, which allowed it to put on unlicensed, and hence uncensored, plays. It should not be confused with the club of the same name in Frith Street that became a haunt of the Kray brothers.

52 Great Newport Street runs east from Charing Cross Road to Upper St. Martin's Lane, and was named after Mountjoy Blount, Earl of Newport.

53 The Church of Christ Scientist was founded by Mary Baker Eddy in 1879 based on the beliefs articulated in her book *Science and Health with Key to the Scriptures*, published in 1875.

never been ill before and doesn't really believe it now. She lies in bed groaning and drinking vast quantities of water. I've made her some soup and have told her to ring up here if she wants anything."

"Oh, well," I said, "if she won't see a doctor that's her funeral. If she'd any sense she'd have sent you to get the nearest doctor and she'd probably be all right by this time. Anyhow, I wasn't intending to eat here, so we'll need to leave a message to ring us up if she calls for you. Will that do?"

Mary said it would do, so I went and got a couple more drinks and left a message that when I'd gone they could get either Mary or myself at *The Gargoyle*,[54] in Dean Street.[55]

When I got back to Mary there was another of these interminable young men talking to her. This one, it appeared, was called Arthur Loftus. He looked very young and very unwell. His face was a pale yellow bud sticking out from the black of his suit.

"Oh, my dear," he was saying to Mary, "you should have seen Stella after you left. She was positively pale green and was she being sick? I've never seen anyone so sick. I said to her, 'Stella, darling, you definitely ought to see a doctor,' but she only shook her head and told me to go to hell. I must say, darling, that her pale green face goes terribly well with her red hair. 'Darling,' I told her, 'you ought to adopt a pale green make up – you've no idea how it suits you.' She did not seem to think very much of the idea, though."

"You are a pig, Arthur," Mary said. "Stella is really very ill indeed. I wonder whether she's eaten anything that disagreed with her? I don't see how she can have done that, because she's had exactly the same as I have and I feel very fit."

I thought that the ghost of the sick Stella was going to settle down on the party, so I managed to shake off the young man and went out with Mary.

It was a very successful evening, everything considered. There was no telephone call for Mary and I got on very well with her. By the end of dinner I knew that I'd got it pretty bad and I didn't care a damn. We danced

54 *The Gargoyle* was a rooftop club popular with artists, writers and radicals, which was founded in 1925 at 69 Dean Street. In the 1940s it was still owned by its founder, the Hon. David Tennant, and sported two Matisse paintings which he had bought in Paris. Todd was a habitué of *The Gargoyle*, and a friend of Tennant.

55 Dean Street lies in Soho and runs south from Oxford Street to Shaftesbury Avenue.

to the music in the mirrored supper room and had a good deal to drink.

By the time *The Gargoyle* closed I was definitely high and it wasn't all drink. I offered to get a taxi to see Mary back to Roger's house in the Square, but as it was a fine and warm autumn evening she said that she'd rather walk. This was all right by me. It meant that the evening was to be prolonged by a little. We didn't hurry, but sauntered along Great Russell Street,[56] past the British Museum,[57] and up Southampton Row.[58] Even though we didn't hurry the time went too quickly for me.

When we got to Mecklenburgh Square I was just about to say good-bye when the door of the house opened. Roger Sharon looked out.

"Oh, it's you Mary, and Max," he said in an anxious voice, "I do wish you'd come and take a look at Stella. She really seems to be most frightfully ill. I don't know what I can do about her. She refuses to let me send for a doctor, says she can't bear them."

I know next to nothing about medicine, beyond the commoner sorts of first-aid, but I've run across a good many doctors in my time and I've picked up some of the jargon and a good deal of odd information.

As soon as I looked at Stella Mortimer I knew she ought to see a proper doctor. She lay in a divan bed in a room which was heated by a Cozy stove.[59] Like all Roger's rooms the walls of this one were painted white. As a result the room looked appallingly cold, and the cold light made her look even worse. She was obviously in considerable pain and there were little white beads of sweat on her forehead. Her hands were clutching at her abdomen.

"Good Lord," I exclaimed, "you really must see a doctor. Roger, go and get a doctor at once."

Roger started towards the door. The girl on the bed raised her head with some effort.

"Roger darling," she spoke between clenched teeth, "if you get a doctor I'll never speak to you again."

56　Great Russell Street is named after the Russell family, who acquired the Bloomsbury Estate through marriage.

57　The British Museum was established by an Act of Parliament in 1753 to house a bequest of over 21,000 objects collected by Sir Hans Sloane.

58　Southampton Row, which runs south from Russell Square, was named after the 4th Earl of Southampton.

59　The Cozy Stove Co. Ltd. operated from 42 Berners Street and manufactured a range of open fire stoves.

He hesitated half way across the room. He looked at me and then at Stella. She won the battle of wills. He came slowly back across the room and stood at the head of the bed, looking down at the girl. His face was clouded with bewilderment, and anxiety.

The door of the room opened and the large bull-head and bulky shoulders of Harold Ironside inserted themselves through the aperture.

"I say, Stella, old girl," he said nervously, glancing at Roger as he spoke, "how are you feeling?"

She twisted her lips into a smile. I don't know how she managed it. If I'd been in the condition in which she was all I'd have squeezed out would have been the most horrifying scowl.

"Oh, it's all right, Harold darling. I'll be better in the morning. I know. I can feel the pain receding."

Roger paid no attention whatsoever to Harold. The ex-wrestler might not have been in the room for all the attention he attracted from his host. Roger's attitude as he looked down at Stella was at once protective and inclined to be possessive.

"I say," I made another effort, "do you think you'll be able to sleep? Can you think of anything you have eaten which might have upset you like this?"

She dealt with the second question first, "No, there is absolutely nothing that I've eaten which could have done this to me. I was down at Linton[60] staying with Mary and we both ate exactly the same the whole time and we've eaten exactly the same ever since we came back. I cannot be suffering from any kind of food poisoning. As for sleeping – well, all I can do is hope to get a little sleep. Roger has some sleeping tablets and he's promised to give me a couple."

I did not like leaving the girl, who was obviously so sick, but it seemed that there was nothing I could do, and I supposed that she would be looked after, to the best of their abilities, by the various members of the household.

I said good-night to Mary and told her that if there was anything I could do I hoped she'd ring me up. Not, I thought, that there was much anyone could do for a girl who refused to see a doctor. I asked Mary if Stella was religious.

"Good Lord, no, Max," she exclaimed in an amused voice, "she's not the least bit religious, but she's got this bee in her bonnet from her parents and she loathes the sight of doctors."

60 Linton is a small village on the border of Cambridgeshire and Essex.

I had to walk almost to Camden Town[61] before I picked up a taxi cruising along. I didn't mind the walk as I wanted to clear my head which was filled with the fumes of foolish dreams.

---

61 Camden Town became important because of its proximity to railways and the Regent's Canal. It was named after the first Earl of Camden and lies to the north of Euston Road.

CHAPTER THREE

UNDER THE WEATHER

I TOLD the old man about Stella's illness and he growled. "Silly little so-an'-so," he said, "she should see a doctor. That's the trouble wi' these cranks – they always know so much better than those who ha' had the trainin'. Bah!"

The subject was more or less dropped as the Professor was doing one of his really intensive bouts of work on the *History of Botany* and this meant that we both stuck with our noses to the grindwheel for a couple of days.

I had known that I was not to see Mary the next night, so I didn't bother to ring her, but I got on the phone fairly early the next morning, at least as early as I judged it was decent to ring an actress who was resting.

Most of the conversation is no concern of anyone but myself. I have said I had got it badly and that should be enough. I was as loving as a pigeon with one squab. But, at the end of the conversation, I said, "Oh, by the way, how's Stella? Recovered from her pains?"

"Oh, yes," Mary replied, "She's feeling ever so much better this morning. The sickness and the rest of it have stopped and so has the pain. Well, I'll see you this evening, darling. At the *Arts* at five-thirty."

When I told the Professor about Stella's recovery he glowered at me over the tops of his glasses and blew out his cheeks.

"I don't like it all," he grumbled, "it's a bad sign. Find out what the girl had bin eatin'. Had she bin havin' mushrooms, for instance? Tell me when ye get in this evening."

The day passed rapidly, in spite of my feeling that it was going to drag. The old man ought to have been a slave driver. He could have made even a mule go. Not that he bullied me at all. The way he gets work out of me is that he drives himself so hard that I feel ashamed at my failure to keep up with him, and so I flog myself up to nearly his level.

I had a very pleasant dinner with Mary and saw her home. I went in with her for a minute to see Stella, who was not asleep. The girl was sitting up in bed and the muscles of her face seemed more relaxed and the tight lines of pain had vanished, but, all the same, she did not look at all well. In fact I have rarely seen anyone who looked so ill.

"Hullo," I said with the feeling that I did not know how to start a conversation, for you cannot congratulate a person who looks like warmed-up death on looking fit. "How are you feeling, and how is the pain?"

"Thank you," she said and her voice was thin and tired, "I feel ever so much better. I can't think what was wrong with me. It was most annoying as I had just arranged to go down to Linton next week to join Mary in the rep, and now it looks as though I won't be fit to go."

Roger had obviously been exercising his incapability for doing any direct good in the purchase of anything that he thought might be of some help to Stella. There were piles of fruit beside her bed, grapes and oranges vied with one another in a seemingly endless profusion, and new novels were piled up, bright in their dust-wrappers. Both the fruit and the novels seemed to be untouched, but there were empty bottles in a neat row, which showed that Roger had done his best to deal with Stella's thirst.

I was just about to say good-night and go away when I remembered what the old man had said.

"I say, Stella," I asked her, "had you been eating mushrooms? Old Professor Stubbs told me to ask you."

"Why, yes," she said, "of course we had been eating mushrooms. Mary and I picked nearly three pounds of them in a water-meadow outside Linton the day before we came up to town, and we brought them with us as a sort of contribution to the housekeeping."

"Oh," I said, "I don't know very much about the poisonous fungi of this country – it's hardly my line – but I'd say that you'd eaten something in mistake for a mushroom."

A puzzled look had suddenly appeared on Stella's face. She began to answer me and changed her mind.

"Anyhow," she said, "I feel a bit better now, and so no harm's been done. But it will be a long time before I eat another mushroom if you really think that that is what has made me so ill." She shuddered as she thought of the pain which she had suffered. "It's lucky that none of the rest got a bit of the poison toadstool, or else we might all have been lying here in bed with no one to help us, for after the party finished we all ate mushrooms on toast."

"If you'd had any sense," I said rather heavily, "you'd have called in a doctor as soon as you felt ill. He might have been able to put a stomach-pump or something on you and have saved you all that trouble. You know you are stupid to let things go. Are you sure you would not like to see a doctor now, just to make sure that you're all right again and that there's no fear of the pain recurring?"

"No," her voice was firm in spite of her weakness, "I do not want to see a doctor. After all, I was right, wasn't I? I got better without the help of a doctor. All a doctor would have done was to keep me in bed and he'd have made me feel much worse than I really was. I *was* right, wasn't I?"

"I wouldn't say you were right," I replied, "rather I'd say you were damned lucky. You might have eaten one of the two or three really poisonous English fungi and then where would you have been?"

I got no answer to this question and I can't say that I expected one. The question was purely rhetorical. I said good-night to Mary and was lucky enough to catch a taxi in Gray's Inn Road.[62]

As I was walking up the stairs to my room I heard a familiar roll of thunder. It was the old man calling me. He had heard me come in. I went into his room. He was in bed, propped up with a mountain of pillows and swathed in his tartan dressing-gown.

He was smoking his filthy little pipe and had a large volume, bound in calf which was desiccated and powdering, propped on the bed in front of him.

"Did ye ask that girl what I told ye?" he demanded fiercely. "Had she bin eatin' mushrooms?"

"As a matter of fact she had," I replied, "but it's all right now. She feels much better and will be about again in a day or two."

The old man glared at me, his grey bushy eyebrows seeming to grow larger as he frowned.

"Oh, the hell o' it," he roared suddenly and started to heave himself out of bed. Books and papers cascaded in an unnoticed flood on to the floor.

He started to dress himself. I think he would have made his fortune as a quick-change artist. While he flung his clothes around him he mumbled at me.

62 Gray's Inn Road runs south from King's Cross to Holburn. Gray's Inn is one of the four Inns of Court, associations to which barristers or judges in England or Wales must belong in order to practice their profession, and is named after Reginald de Grey of Winton.

"Max, sometimes I think ye're a bloody fool, but then, o' course, ye can't be expected to know everythin' or if ye do know it, to call it to yer mind just at the moment when it's wanted. Did ye never hear of a fungus called *Amanita phalloides*,[63] eh?"

Now I thought of it I remembered that I did know *Amanita phalloides* which commonly goes by the name of the Death Cap. I also remembered that the damned thing was supposed to be responsible for about ninety per cent. of the deaths caused by eating poisonous fungi.

"Yes," I said, "I remember it all right. But I don't think there's any need to worry. If Stella has eaten a bit of the thing she's certainly been very ill, but she is now recovering."

"Um," he grunted at me as he tied his shoe-laces, "that's just the trouble. Ye can't be expected to know the clinical symptoms o' poisoning by *Amanita* but one o' the commonest is that the victim has hellish abdominal pains an' vomitin' an' diarrhoea, an' that these symptoms do not come on for about twelve hours after eatin' the dam' thin'. That's why I was kinda worried when ye described the girl's symptoms to me, an' why I asked ye for details about what she'd bin eatin'. Then ye come home an' ye tell me that she's feelin' much better. Bah! There ye are again – *Amanita* or I'm a cock-eyed scarecrow. There's usually a quiet period after two days an' then the symptoms return. Whether she likes it or not, she's goin' to see a doctor an' I'm goin' to collect him as quickly as I dam' well can. Go an' get the car out an' I'll phone Nick Roberts. He's the one feller I know well who might be able to do somethin'. We'll collect him on the way."

By this time the urgency of the thing had got me, so I did not even protest at the thought of the aged Bentley[64] roaring through the night streets of London. Normally I would have suggested a taxi, but I could see that argument would get me nowhere. I went and withdrew the old man's chariot from its stable.

I had not had time to do more than get it out and move myself from the driving seat into the seat beside it before the old man came hurtling from the house, as if he had been expelled by some immense catapult of the sort used for throwing planes off ships at sea.

---

63 *Amanita phalloides*, or the Death Cap, was first described by the French botanist Sébastien Vaillant (1669-1722).
64 Walter Owen Bentley (1888-1971) built his first Bentley engine in 1919 in New Street Mews, now Chagford Street, and sold his first car in 1921.

Although he is so heavily built the Professor moves quickly when he wants to, and this was one of the times when he most certainly wanted to. He swung the car round, to the immense peril of a lamp standard, and we roared up the hill into Hampstead High Street and then on down Fitzjohn's Avenue.[65] We turned down one of the side turnings which lead to Finchley Road.[66] Half way down the Professor pulled up with a jerk that nearly threw me through the windscreen. We did not need to wait. As the car stopped a door opened and a man came out of it, a thin man with a serious face who looked as though he had never been thinking of bed but was just about to set out on a professional visit. He carried a rather larger bag than I associated with the average doctor. He was quite unhurried, a contrast to the rushing progress of Professor Stubbs.

"Good evening, John," he said, and his voice was slow and pleasant, "I hope you haven't brought me out at this time of night on a wild goose chase."

"Wild goose chase be blanketed," roared the old man, "just you listen to this!"

He ran quickly through the story which I had related, with his own deduction from it. "Well," he bellowed, "d'ye think I'm right in takin' a serious view o' the matter?"

Dr. Roberts climbed into the car and nodded slowly. "Hmm," he said, "I don't think there's any doubt, John, that you are right. We'll just need to hope that we are in time. If only that girl had called in a doctor when she was first ill things would have been easier. Any doctor in his senses would recognise that period before the oncome of the symptoms. It's almost diagnostic of *Amanita* poisoning."

Professor Stubbs slammed his gears and we started off again with the vigour of a charger rushing into battle. We roared through Swiss Cottage[67]

---

65 Fitzjohn's Avenue was named after one of the country homes of the Maryon-Wilson family, who had owned the manorial estate on which it was built. *Harper's Magazine* described the tree-lined and elegant avenue as "one of the noblest streets" in the world in 1883.

66 Originally called Finchley New Road, this was a turnpike road built under the *Finchley Road Act* of 1826 to provide an easier route from central London to Hampstead.

67 Swiss Cottage takes it name from an inn built in the style of a Swiss chalet in 1804.

and on to Lord's.[68] At Baker Street[69] we missed a belated taxi by the fraction of an inch and streams of profanity from the startled driver failed to perturb the old man, who held on to the wheel as if it was the bucking wheel of a windjammer in a hurricane.

At the end of Euston Road,[70] he shot through a set of traffic lights which were against him. A policeman pulled him up. The old man just glared at him and howled, "I'm drivin' a doctor to see a patient who's kinda seriously ill. If ye want me, ye can get me later. Or," a bright idea struck him, "ring up Chief Inspector Bishop at the Yard an' ye'll find he'll swear I'm all right."

Before the policeman had time to take this in, the Professor had started off again and we careered on like a lunatic circus. I turned my head to see how Dr. Roberts was taking this madcap ride. He sat bolt upright in the back, and, judging from his face, he might have been sitting in the back of a Rolls Royce, purring quietly along at the hands of a first-class chauffeur. I must say I envied him his extreme composure. What the old man's driving does to my metabolism won't bear thinking about.

I showed the old man which of the remaining houses in the bomb-damaged Mecklenburgh Square[71] belonged to Roger Sharon and we drew up in front of it. There was still light showing from some of the windows. The old man pressed the electric bell with a shove that nearly drove it through the stucco surface of the porch.

The door was opened by Roger himself. He looked at the old man in some surprise and then he saw that I was there too. I took control of the situation and walked in, followed by the Professor and Dr. Roberts.

68 Lord's is home to the Marylebone Cricket Ground, and is named after Thomas Lord, the ground's founder.

69 Baker Street runs south from Regent's Park towards Oxford Street and is, of course, best known as the street in which Sherlock Holmes lived.

70 Euston Road was opened as part of the New Road in 1756. It runs east to west from Marylebone to Pentonville Road and provides access to St Pancras, Euston and King's Cross Stations.

71 Two high explosive bombs are known to have been dropped on the area between October 1940 and June 1941. There was also a flying bomb in the Spring of 1944, and this one caused Todd to vacate no. 18 and move to Essex. The back wall of no. 18 was damaged, and Todd's pillow and mattress were penetrated by splinters of glass. Fortunately, at the time he had been spending the night with David and Virginia Tennant in their flat below *The Gargoyle*, and only found out the next day.

"Look here, Roger," I said, putting as much urgency as possible into my voice, "I told Professor Stubbs about Stella's illness and he said that whether she likes doctors or not she's got to see one. He thinks, and Dr. Roberts, who is an expert on the subject, agrees with him, that Stella's suffering from mushroom poisoning. From poisoning by one of the most deadly fungi – called the Death Cap. You've *got* to persuade her to see Dr. Roberts. It may be her only chance."

Roger looked at us doubtfully, but realised that we were in deadly earnest.

"Well," he said slowly, leading us into the large room where he had held his party, "I'll see what I can do."

"Tell her, Roger," I urged, "that it wasn't your fault at all that there is a doctor here. Make it clear that it's my fault. Say I'm the sort of chap that's always shoving his nose into other people's business, Tell her what you damn well like, but make certain that she will see Dr. Roberts and that she will co-operate with him."

"All right," Roger did not seem to be at all happy about the business, "I'll do what I can. But, you see Max, she's been feeling so much more restful this evening that she believes that her constitution has thrown off anything that was wrong with her."

"Mr. Sharon," the doctor's voice was firm, "I do not think that there is any harm in frightening her, under the circumstances. You can make it quite clear to her that one of the worst and most dangerous periods in poisoning from *Amanita phalloides* is that of quiescence which is apt to appear after two days. Make it quite clear to her that, if she will not see me, she is in grave danger of the symptoms reappearing in a very much more intense form, which may actually result in her death."

"Death?" Roger's fact went rather pale, "you don't mean that she's in any real danger, do you?"

"I mean just that, Mr. Sharon. If Miss Mortimer is suffering from *Amanita* poisoning, I am afraid that there is nothing more probable than that she may die of it. I am willing to do all that I can, but I am not a miracle worker, and I have not been called in until very late."

"But she can't die," Roger was foolishly repeating the phrase to himself while the doctor spoke, "she can't die. She can't die. She's so alive."

"Well, Mr. Sharon, I have been blunt. I will be even more blunt. If as I suspect, Miss Mortimer is suffering from this poison, her only chance, and it is a bare chance, is in seeing me immediately."

"Come on, man," the old man broke in gruffly, "you go an' do as ye're told. Maybe old Nick here will be able to help her out of the mess. We'll wait here till ye've had a chance to argue with her."

The Professor's eyes were questing round the room while he spoke. They lightened as he saw a row of a dozen quart bottles of Tolly.[72]

"In the meantime," he said, "d'ye mind if I help meself to some o' yer beer. It's thirsty work drivin' in the middle o' the night."

"Help yourself to anything you like," Roger replied, with a gesture towards his various bottles of drink. He left the room.

The old man stumped across to the table and grabbed a pint mug and a couple of bottles. He sat down on a couch and started to demolish them. I went and poured a more modest pint for myself. The doctor accepted a small glass of sherry.

I was just about to start the conversation when the door of the room opened. It was Mary. She was wearing an electric flash blue dressing-gown and she looked wonderful. My heart leapt into my throat and collided with the gulp of beer I had just taken. I choked. When I had recovered I performed the necessary introductions.

"But, Max darling," she said when I had explained the reason for our midnight visit, "I'm quite sure that neither Stella nor myself would have picked a poison toadstool among the mushrooms. You see Stella has that little King Penguin book on poisonous fungi[73] and we both know the pictures in it. Stella was terribly interested in these sort of things and she told me that once, at the beginning of the war, when she was still a schoolgirl, she tried to see how many different sorts of dishes she could get off Hampstead Heath.[74] She showed me a little book by a man called Jason Hill all about the wild foods of Britain. I can't remember all that she said

---

72 Tollemache's Breweries Ltd. were formed when Tollemache's Ipswich Brewery acquired Collier Brothers of Walthamstow in 1920. "Tolly for quality" was one of their pre-war slogans.

73 King Penguins were a series of pocket-sized, attractively illustrated books published by Penguin Books between 1939 and 1955. *Poisonous Fungi* by John Ramsbottom, and illustrated by Rose Ellenby, was published in 1945 and was the twenty-third in the series.

74 Hampstead Heath is the wildest of London's parks and is home to over 350 different types of fungi and numerous plants. Todd lived on the edge of Hampstead Heath when he was first married.

she ate off Hampstead Heath, but I remember that there were quite a lot of things. She wouldn't have made a mistake like that."

"Um," the old man growled, "it looks mighty like as though she had made a mistake. Ye know, if ye're in a hurry, there's not an almighty difference between *Amanita* an' the common mushroom, when they're both of 'em very young. Tell me, were ye tryin' to choose button mushrooms when ye picked 'em?"

"Naturally. They are so much nicer than the fully grown ones. All the same I don't see how Stella could have made a mistake. You see she and Douglas Newsome cooked the supper together, mushrooms on toast."

"But look here," I interrupted, "Douglas was as drunk as a coot. He wouldn't have been much good as a cook. When I left he was sleeping it off on this sofa."

"Oh, but, Max darling, haven't you noticed how quickly Douglas recovers if he's allowed to sleep?"

I didn't know Douglas Newsome all that well and I said so. I also said that if he had been drunk he might have made a mistake which Stella would not have done. He might have peeled the Death Cap and put it on to cook.

Mary did not seem at all convinced, but she finally allowed that I might be right. Looking at Dr. Roberts I could see that I had made my point. He nodded his head wisely at me.

The old man had found a cigar in his pocket. It looked rather battered but he repaired the mouth-end of it with a bit of stamp-paper and proceeded to smoke it. It had a bend in the middle which helped to give his face an incredibly rakish effect.

I wandered down the room and started talking to Mary. She seemed to be very worried about Stella. She was blaming herself for not having insisted on her friend seeing a doctor. I pointed out that it was not her fault, and that she could not in any way consider herself to blame for the state of affairs, but she took no comfort from my words. She seemed to be determined to put herself in the wrong.

CHAPTER FOUR

THE BRIGHT FACE OF DEATH

ROGER OPENED the door and came in. His face was ashy white, the white of wood which has been burned. He took out a handkerchief and wiped his forehead.

"It's all right, Dr. Roberts," he said, "she'll see you now."

The doctor and Professor Stubbs rose to their feet and followed Roger. I was about to go after them when the old man turned and gestured to me to stay where I was. For a moment I felt annoyed, for where one botanist can go another should be able to go as well, but then I remembered that, in addition to all his other distinctions, the Professor does happen to be a Doctor of Medicine, though I doubt if he has practised since he put a splint on Noah as he came out of the Ark. I let them go and turned towards Roger.

"My God, Max," he said, "you've no idea what you let me in for by arriving here with a doctor. Where the subject of doctors is concerned I have never met anyone who is so unreasonable as Stella. She was quite convinced that I had organised a plot with you – I'm sure she'll never speak to you again as long as she lives. I tried frightening her, but it wasn't any good. I don't think she is frightened of the thought of death. She is so much alive herself that she cannot make the imaginative effort necessary to understand what it means to be dead. In the end I asked her to marry me."

"What?" Mary dropped her glass and a long dark splash ran down the front of her dressing-gown, "You asked her to marry you, Roger dear? I didn't think you wanted to marry."

"Oh, I don't know," Roger was uneasy, "She seemed as astonished as you are. Then she asked for a little time to think it over. I said all right if she'd see the doctor first, and, rather to my surprise she agreed to see him."

It seemed that the room was in for another party, for as time went on the rest of the household drifted in. Harold Ironside was the first. Like Roger he was fully dressed. He remained as far from Roger as he possibly could. His beaten face looked as though it had been suddenly mauled by the scythe of Old Father Time[75] himself. Long grey creases ran down the sides of his mouth and across his forehead. He sat on the edge of an armchair, idly twisting a piece of paper and tearing it into the shape of a ballerina doll. I had not realised how skilful and gentle these huge hands could be. He seemed to be working quite absent-mindedly, but the doll was as exquisite as if it had been made in hours of hard and conscious work. He stood the ballerina up on the arm of his chair and flicked her idly with his finger. She pirouetted in the air and then fell unregarded to the floor.

Douglas Newsome and Arthur Loftus came in together. They looked at Roger and Harold doubtfully.

"How is she?" asked Douglas, wandering over to the table and grabbing hold of a bottle of whisky. Nobody replied to him. He came over and sat beside me.

"I say, Max," he whispered confidentially, "what's all the cuffuffle about? I was sleeping the sleep of the just, those who have had just a drop too much whisky, but the noise of people tramping about woke me. Is Stella any worse?"

I told him what I had done in the way of bringing along the old man and Dr. Roberts. He shook his head sadly.

"Poor Stella won't like that," he said portentously, "she doesn't like doctors. As a matter of fact," his voice dropped to a whisper, "I can't say I like them myself. They do such embarrassing things to one, don't they? Nothing is sacred to a doctor. He just pulls, pokes and pries wherever he thinks fit."

Arthur Loftus wrapped in a scarlet flannel dressing-gown was perched on the arm of the couch, next to Mary. I can't say I liked having him there. I was rather astonished to find that I was beginning to develop possessive instincts about her. This wasn't any too good. It meant that my fall was more serious than usual. As a rule I'm happy enough to let others talk to my girl and even take her out to dinner, when I'm not around. Now I found that the pale presence of Mr. Loftus was getting on my nerves. I think the reason for this was that I'm not at all up in the theatre. I like

75 Old Father Time is also the name given to a weather vane at Lord's cricket ground which depicts Father Time, with his scythe, removing the bails from a set of stumps. It was wrenched from its position on the Grand Stand by a barrage balloon in 1941, the only casualty of the Second World War at Lord's.

actresses but that is all. I don't know all the nicknames and the jargon. Arthur Loftus knew it all. It struck me, but I was prejudiced, that he was just the sort of young man who would be *au fait* with all the latest slang and the hottest gossip. I don't think I liked him at all.

Alec Dolittle suddenly appeared in the room. He was wearing a pair of pyjamas which were almost indecently too small for him. He had not bothered to put on a dressing-gown, if he possessed one. He stood in the doorway, rubbing his eyes sleepily.

It was quite a family party. Anyone who felt like a drink just went across and helped themselves. I noticed that everyone felt that they wanted a drink. Most of them seemed to want it pretty badly. I stuck to beer myself.

Quite unexpectedly there was a hush in the room. Mary suddenly spoke at the top of her voice. I could have slapped her if I hadn't loved her so much.

"Oh but, Arthur dear, you don't know the latest. You're miles behind the times. Roger has just asked Stella to marry him!"

I happened to be looking straight at Harold Ironside. His large red hands slowly contracted into large white balls. He leaned forward and slowly, very slowly, lifted himself out of the seat. It seemed to me that I was watching a slow motion film. All Harold's actions had that same curiously exaggerated quality. He straightened himself up and looked across at Roger.

"Is that true, Roger?" he asked in a mild voice. Roger looked up at him and nodded his head. Harold turned very slowly and went towards the door. For a moment I thought he was not going to bother to open it but was just about to attempt to push his way right through it. However, he reached out one hand and grasped the knob. He turned his huge ugly face towards the room.

"Good-night, everyone," he said, and he was gone. I could hear his heavy yet soft footsteps outside. No one said anything for a moment.

"I'm sorry you said that, Mary," Roger remarked, looking up at her. "I didn't mean to tell anyone until she had either accepted me or turned me down."

I will say that for Mary. She looked penitent. Her face was so beautiful that I wanted to reach out and pick it like a magnolia flower.

"I'm most frightfully sorry, Roger dear," she said, "I didn't know there was any secret about it and Arthur was telling me all the latest. He always knows the latest, so I thought I'd give him a surprise by telling him something he didn't know."

Roger laughed. His laugh was not a happy laugh, nor even an amused one. He sounded thoroughly unhappy.

"I say, Max," he turned to me, "I wonder how much longer they'll be. They've been the hell of a time already, haven't they? Do you think I should go and offer to lend a hand? I'm sure there must be *something* I could do to help, don't you agree?"

"No," I said, "Let them alone. The old man knows his onions all right and I believe that Dr. Roberts is the very best man you could have got to look after Stella. If there is anything that can be done, he'll do it. Don't look so worried, old man, I think that quite a lot of what the doctor said to you was said with the intention of frightening you so that you'd frighten Stella into seeing him. I'm sure she'll be all right."

This just went to show how wrong I was. We went on sitting in the room for a time which seemed to be interminable. The next time the door opened it was the old man himself. He gestured to me and I rose and went out. His heavy face was serious and he looked worried.

"See here, Max," he said in a bumbling whisper, "what I have to say is for yer own ears alone. Don't ye go spreadin' it about. That girl is in a bad way an' I don't mind admittin' it. All the thunderin' symptoms have recurred, in an intensified form. Speakin' personally, I'd say she was a goner. Even Roberts seems afraid that she ain't got a hope in hell o' pullin' through. But he won't chuck it up. Trust Nick for that. He's as tough as a ten year old cockerel. He'll fight for her every inch o' the way. He has bin dealin' with her gently, an' the only thin' he's said in the way of a reproach is 'Ye should ha' called me in as soon as ye became ill. Me job 'ud ha' bin easier then.' There's nothin' anyone can do that ain't bein' done."

When I went back into the room the others looked at me expectantly.

"Oh," I said, thinking quickly and lying glibly, "the old man had mislaid his lighter and wondered if I had some matches. He wants to smoke his pipe. He didn't want to come in as he was afraid of being questioned, but he says that Stella is as well as can be expected."

There was a silence in the room which was oppressive in its unnatural heaviness. I thought I heard Stella's voice raised in pain and rose to my feet.

"I say, Roger," I ventured, "do you mind if I play the gramophone? We are none of us doing any good by sitting here and moping."

Roger signified that he didn't mind if I played the gramophone or if I took the machine and dumped it in the middle of the Red Sea. I got up and placed a record on the turn-table.

The gramophone was no help. The silences that filled the gaps between the records were worse than the continual buzzing silence had been.

Mary was talking to Douglas Newsome. He kept on glancing across at me as they spoke. I wondered what they were talking about. I made a final effort at the gramophone and put on a record of Louis Armstrong[76] singing *Ain't Misbehavin'*.[77] When the record finished I replenished my glass and wandered back to my seat. Mary and Douglas made room for me between them.

Douglas turned round to me. His face looked rather puzzled.

"Mary says that Stella must have eaten some of the mushrooms we cooked together. I don't see that. I ate the mushrooms too and I'm not the least bit poisoned. Never felt fitter in my life. I'll admit that I was slightly tight," he said with the air of one referring to a rare occurrence, "but I prepared the mushrooms for Stella who was cooking and they all peeled. Poison toadstools don't peel. I know that. My mother told me."

I mightn't have been very bright upon the subject of poison fungi up till that moment, but here I knew what I was talking about. It was one of the favourite beliefs which had no foundation in any sort of fact.

"Douglas," I was as gentle as possible, "if you tell me that it did not turn the silver spoons black I will scream. The idea that only non-poisonous fungi can be peeled is as extinct as the dodo, or rather more so. It stinks worse than all the bones in history. Whether a fungus can be peeled or not depends entirely on the nature of that fungus, its formation and so on. All the *Amanita* peel just as well as the ordinary field mushroom. You cannot tell a poison fungus from a non-poisonous one by any test whatsoever."

I could see that he did not believe me, but I really did not feel that it was the right time of night for me to start on the psychological basis of his character, destroying his belief in what he had heard from his mother.

The horrible waiting silence went on. I could look out of the long windows into the Square. I was surprised to realise that the dawn was lighting

76 Louis Armstrong (1901-1971) was a jazz trumpeter and singer who was a major influence on popular music.

77 *Ain't Misbehavin'* was written by Fats Waller, Harry Brooks and Andy Razaf in 1929; Louis Armstrong released a recording the same year.

the grey roof of the war-time air-raid shelter[78] in the garden.

The door opened quite quietly. I looked up expecting to see the old man. It was not him, however, but Dr. Roberts.

This was not the Dr. Roberts who had arrived at the house, looking as if he was going to do his rounds in a hospital or going to call on a patient; the Dr. Roberts of the imperturbable manner and the perfect grooming.

He stood in the door in his shirt sleeves, which were rolled up above his elbows. His tie had come adrift from his collar and the top button was undone. His hair was lank and dark with sweat.

Roger rose to his feet. Behind the doctor I could see the enormous figure of Harold Ironside. Before anyone had time to say anything the doctor spoke.

"I am very sorry to have to admit it," he said, "but I am afraid I have failed. Your friend is dying. I hope you will accept my assurances that I have done everything possible. I was too late."

---

78 The most common domestic air-raid shelter was the Anderson shelter, named after Sir John Anderson, which was built of panels of galvanised corrugated steel and which could accommodate up to six people.

CHAPTER FIVE

MEDICAL CORONER

ALTHOUGH I had been with Professor Stubbs for a considerable time I had never attended an inquest before. The small room was not very crowded. Apart from the people I knew there were only one or two members of the public, who looked as though they had nothing to do and enjoyed doing it to the best of their abilities. Of course there were the usual handful of tired looking and thoroughly bored reporters.

The coroner's name was Mountjoy, Dr. Mountjoy. I have rarely seen an individual with such an unjoyful face. He looked as though the whole world had turned sour on him.

I was attending the inquest partly as Mary's escort and partly as the Professor's assistant, for the old man had insisted on coming along. It was not expected that there would be very much fuss about the affair.

The old man told me that he knew the coroner. The way he told me made me feel that he did not think that there was much good to be said for him.

The preliminaries, evidence of identification, of the cause of death and so on, were quickly passed over. Then the coroner looked at a sheet of paper before him. "Mary Winstone," he said, pursing his thin lips with a gesture of distaste.

"Miss Winstone? Yes? You are an actress I believe? Yes? Now you say that you gathered the mushrooms with your friend. Can you tell me whose suggestion this was?"

"Oh, it was Stella's – I mean Miss Mortimer's idea. I'm afraid I don't know enough about such things."

"Considering how things have turned out, Miss Winstone," the voice was dry, "I don't think that is a very bad thing, do you?"

Mary sobbed. I wanted to get up and bat the coroner a hard one.

"Mmm, yes, Miss Winstone, you brought these 'mushrooms' up to town with you, as a contribution to the larder of the friend with whom you were both staying. Now can you tell me something about the actual – ah – consumption of these delectable morsels?"

For a moment I thought Mary was looking puzzled, but I quickly realised that she was trying to organise her thoughts.

"Well, we had a party in the evening and there were a lot of people there. After they had all gone away Stella said she'd make mushrooms on toast. Mr. Newsome offered to help her. So we all had some. That's all."

The coroner made one or two notes and then, as if suddenly realising his delay, dismissed Mary. Douglas Newsome was next on the list. The coroner asked him to give his own account of the proceedings.

"Well," his voice was rather confidential, "to tell you the truth, I'm afraid that I'd had a drop too much to drink. However, I'd had a good hour or so's sleep and was feeling a bit better. When Stella said she'd make something to eat I thought I might as well weigh in with an offer to play scullion. She set me to the job of peeling the mushrooms. I peeled every blinking," the coroner scowled at him, "I beg your pardon, I peeled every single mushroom there was in the house. If you've never tried peeling mushrooms you don't know how long it takes you."

"When I wish for your comments, Mr. – mm – Newsome," the coroner was acid, "I will ask you for them."

"All right, cock," Douglas was unabashed and the coroner's clerk looked almost as scandalised as that worthy himself. Douglas let his long thin face relax into his usual sadness of expression and stood waiting. It seemed to be a dead-lock, for he had nothing more to say and the coroner couldn't think of a question.

The coroner gave Roger Sharon hell for his failure to call a doctor. I could see that the Professor beside me was getting pretty restive. I don't know how he had managed to wangle things so that he was called in evidence, but he was.

The coroner, looked at his untidy, ash-besprinkled bulk with a look that said he had rarely seen anyone he disliked so much.

"Mr. Stubbs?" he said, with a seemingly intentional stress on the Mister part of the question.

"Ye can take it that way if ye like, son," the old man was as amiable as a summer day. "Or ye can call me Doc. or Prof. I ain't what ye call fussy."

"Ah, yes," the coroner ruffled his papers fussily, "I believe you have the right to call yourself Doctor. I presume you are a Doctor of Philosophy or of Science?"[79]

"Yes," the old man was mild. He left the question there. The coroner adjusted a pair of horn rimmed spectacles.

"You, I gather from the notes at my disposal, were sufficiently familiar with the symptoms of poisoning by fungi to identify the cause of Miss Mortimer's illness when it was described to you by your assistant?"

"Uhhuh," the old man nodded his head heavily. His grey hair wagged on the top of his head.

"How does it come that you, a layman, should be so familiar with the symptoms of a comparatively rare condition?"

"Oh, I dunno," the old man waved his hand in the air, "I just kinda make it me business to know thin's. Got a mind like the lumber room at the top o' a house – never throw anythin' away – it may come in useful one o' these days."[80]

The coroner sniffed. It did not seem that he was impressed by the thought of the old man's mind. Speaking personally, I can say that the Professor's description of his mind was accurate. He's one of the few people I know who never gets less than ninety per cent. in these questionnaires set in Sunday newspapers.

"So, you took it that your suppositions were likely to be correct enough to justify your calling a man of the eminence of Dr. Nicholas Roberts out in the middle of the night?"

The old man drew himself up in the witness place; you could hardly call it a box. He blew out his cheeks and glared at Dr. Mountjoy.

"See, here, son," he said, and his voice was still comparatively mild, "I'd just like to know what ye're up to. Are ye breakin' a lance[81] on behalf o' the medical profession o' this country, or are ye tryin' to investigate the death o'

79 In the United Kingdom a Doctor of Science is a higher doctorate, generally conferred on an individual for exceptional and internationally recognised scholarship.

80 Compare this with Sherlock Holmes in *The Five Orange Pips*: "I say now, as I said then, that a man should keep his little brain attic stocked with all the furniture that he is likely to use, and the rest he can put away in the lumber-room of his library, where he can get it if he wants it."

81 i.e. engaging in a contest, referring to a tilt at a jousting tournament.

this unfortunate girl? I'd just like to know, as if it's the former I think there are one or two things which you ought to know." I wagged my finger at him in admonition but he ignored it. "Firstly I think ye should know that I'm as much o' a thunderin' doctor as ye are, an' ye can look me up in yer directory an' find me when ye get home. An' secondly I'd like to say that it's dam' fool dunderheads like you that make people mistrust the medical profession. God, man, I wouldn't trust you to give me a laxative."

The coroner's thin throat looked as though it had suddenly come to life. Little cords jumped into prominence. I thought he was about to burst. Just before he managed to get himself going however, one of the officers of the court handed him a little scrap of paper, very carefully folded. From where I sat I could see that the word URGENT was scrawled on it in capital letters. The coroner scowled at it. For a moment I thought he was going to throw it away, then he opened it. He took out a clean handkerchief and wiped his glasses. Then he looked up at the old man.

"I beg your pardon, Professor Stubbs," he said politely, "I didn't know who you were. That is all."

"Bah!" roared the old man, getting the last word in, "Ye didn't know who I was, eh? An' ye thought ye'd bullyrag me, eh? Bah! sir, to you an' your court."

I looked around the room to see where the note had come from. It must have been somebody pretty important to have had that effect on the self important and pompous coroner.

Seated beside the door, with his eyes half closed, was a very familiar figure. It was none other than Chief Inspector Bishop. He seemed to be thoroughly bored with the proceedings and gave no answer to my sign of recognition.

I noticed that the coroner was also looking anxiously at the large and well-fed Chief Inspector. As a result of that imposing presence the rest of the proceedings ran smoothly and without trouble.

The coroner delivered a few words on the matter of people who did not call in their doctors early enough. Half way through these the Professor gave a sound that was half way between a grunt and a snore. It shook the coroner, but he managed to get through to the end.

The verdict was, as everyone had expected, Death by Misadventure,[82]

82 i.e. an accidental death not caused by any violation of law or criminal negligence.

with a rider added to the effect that people should take greater care about the fungi they eat.

As we left the court, Bishop bore down on us. He looked very sleepy indeed.

"Oh, no, John," he greeted the old man, "you don't get away as easily as all that."

"Why, what ha' I bin doin'?" the old man howled, with a face that depicted injured innocence. "I bin doin' nothin'. I bin helpin' out, an' I bin doin' me bit tryin' to clean up a coroner's court." His face became gleeful. "Did ye see how I led him up the blinkin' garden path an' then let him have it, eh?"

"Yes, I saw." The Chief Inspector was not encouraging. "If you are not careful you'll find yourself in trouble, not that I suppose that would be anything new for you. But that is not the only bone I have to pick with you. There's a little matter of traffic lights[83] in the Euston Road."

"Traffic lights?" the Professor looked as though he had never heard of them.

"Yes," the Chief Inspector was insultingly patient, "sticks with black and white stripes and three coloured lights at the top, which can be taken as green meaning go, red stop and amber caution. You went on the red, and, not content with that you had the damned effrontery to tell the constable who, very properly, halted you, that I would answer for your sins."

"Oh that," the old man replied with the air of one digging a long way and coming up with an almost forgotten fact, "Oh, that. Well, you see I was in a bit of a hurry at the time an' I didn't want to waste time. Ye see, I couldn't think o' anythin' else to say, an' I really was in a hurry."

"Oh all right," the Chief Inspector gave it up, and smiled at the old man. "I know you were in a hurry and you could probably plead that you were on an errand of mercy. When I saw that you were mixed up with the Mortimer girl's death I thought I should come along and see what kind of funny business you were up to. You know, it's my considered opinion that neither you nor Max should be allowed out without a guardian. However, this time it looks as though there was nothing to deal with but an unfortunate accident."

83 Traffic lights were invented by railway engineer John Peake Knight (1828-1886) and were first installed in London, in 1868, outside the Houses of Parliament.

"Uhhuh," the old man nodded, "it's quite clearly an accident. It might have happened to anyone, but it seems extra hard that it should ha' happened to a girl who knew somethin' about the country an' about the wild foods o' the countryside. Tell me, Max," he turned towards me, "why were there no relations at the inquest. You know these people better than I do."

"I asked Mary," I replied, "if there were any relatives to be told about the tragedy, but she said no. Stella's father was killed in the Blitz and her mother married an American colonel and is now in the United States. Mary said that she would write to her. She thinks Stella has an old aunt somewhere in Somerset, but no one knows how to get hold of her."

Walking down the road ahead of us was Harold Ironside. His huge bull-head was sunk between his broad shoulders and his hands were deep in his pockets. He looked about as miserable as I have ever seen anyone look. The very movement of his feet upon the pavement seemed to express his depression.

The Professor and Chief Inspector Bishop went off together. I made no excuses and managed to escape. I went after Mary who was walking along slowly with Roger Sharon. I had to run a bit to catch them up.

It was difficult to think what I should say to Roger. It had been difficult ever since he had announced his proposal of marriage to Stella. I did not know whether to treat him as a sort of widower. The trouble was that I could not make up my mind as to whether he had really been in love with Stella, or whether he was just carrying his ideas on the subject of hospitality to their logical extreme. After all he had tried every other way of making her see a doctor before he thought of that one.

Against the idea that he was just being the perfect host was his horror at the thought of her death. He seemed to be really deeply cut by it. More deeply than Mary was, for instance, and I knew how fond Mary had been of Stella. It is impossible to compare two men as different as Roger and Harold, but so far as I could make out they were both equally and as deeply hurt.

"That coroner was a brute, wasn't he?" I said when I caught up with them, more by way of making conversation than for any other reason. They agreed with me and we wandered off in search of a teashop. Roger was very silent during tea and rather cramped me. If he hadn't been there, there would have been a lot I could have said to Mary, and if he'd been at all talkative I could have treated the tea as a social occasion. The way things were it was a flop.

Mary was going back to Linton the next day, so I asked her if she would come out for the evening. She said she couldn't, as she had to go and visit relatives.

I went back to Hampstead feeling pretty sour. The old man had got home before me and, having decided that there was nothing in Stella's death which needed his attention, was engaged in making notes on some of his evening primroses.

The next couple of days passed in a pretty hard bout of work, for the old man had to go to a provincial university to deliver some lecture and that meant that he had to prepare it beforehand. This sort of preparation had become one of the banes of my life.

For about a day and half he would write lectures, putting the jokes in the right places, and getting them word perfect. He would stride up and down the room reading from the pages I typed out for him at the top of his voice. Then he would go to deliver the lecture. As sure as God made little apples he would forget to take the nice clean typescript with him; he would dig wildly through all his pockets, shake his head sadly and deliver a very much better lecture without preparation, and with better jokes all in the right places.

Sometimes, in between the chunks of work which I do for the old man – rather like the filling in a sponge cake – I manage to do a bit of work for myself, but not often. I'm writing this book, for instance, in the small hours of the morning, because I can't manage it during the decent hours when normal people manage to do their work. Maybe the old man's habit of working all night is catching, because it seems to me I'm getting the habit too.

The only thought that cheered me was the hope that I would see Mary during the week-end. She had promised to ring me if she was able to get up to town. Unfortunately, she rang me on the Saturday evening and said she'd be unable to make it. This made me feel so low that I could have crawled under a snake. I went out to have a drink.

CHAPTER SIX

THE BLACK BAT NIGHT

Propping up the bar of *The Wheatsheaf*[84] in Rathbone Place[85] I found Douglas Newsome. He looked very unhappy, but that did not make much impression on me, as he always looked as though someone had stolen away the penny world he built himself. I bought him a Scotch Ale.[86]

His conversation was not encouraging. In fact it was difficult to get a reply from him, but that did not worry me much, as I was feeling a bit taciturn myself. The evening dragged slightly.

After a while I began to feel that it might be good if I went and found some more cheerful company. I got up and started to say good-night to Douglas. To my surprise, for I knew he had some money and wasn't trying to borrow at the moment, he rose and followed me out.

"I say, Max," he began rather defensively, "your boss, Professor Stubbs?"

"Yes, what about him?" I was slightly impatient.

"Would he see me if I called on him? If I went to Hampstead now, for instance?"

"Why, what do you want to see him about? Is there anything that I can do? The old man's pretty busy, you know."

"Well, you must understand that I'm not certain, but there's something I feel I should tell the police or someone about. It's about Stella's death."

I looked at him in astonishment. "Look here, Douglas," I said, "you

---

84 *The Wheatsheaf* was one of the watering holes that, in the 1940s, had taken over from *The Fitzroy Tavern* as a venue of choice in Fitzrovia for many bohemian and literary figures.

85 Rathbone Place is named after Captain Rathbone, who constructed buildings here in the early part of the 18th century.

86 Scotch Ale is the name given to a strong bottled beer that was usually brewed for the export market, particularly Belgium and France.

were at the inquest. You heard the verdict of Misadventure. You can't mean that you think there was anything wrong with that, do you? And if you do, what was it?"

He leaned towards me secretively. "Ah," he whispered, "that's just it. I didn't remember this thing till afterwards. That's why I want to see your boss. He'll tell me if it's nonsense and will be easier to deal with than the police. I'd rather not say anything till I see him. Will you take me to see him now?"

I tried to find out what idea it was that was gnawing at his mind. He wouldn't tell me. I suppose I have as big a share of good healthy curiosity as the next chap, so I took Douglas out to see the old man.

Professor Stubbs was sitting in his immense armchair in front of the fire. His after dinner cigar, large and vile, was swathing him with bluish grey smoke, and he held a quart china tankard of beer in his hand. He was reading White's *Animal Cytology*.[87]

He looked up as we came in and inserted a scrap of paper into the book to mark his place before he rose to pour out a pint for each of us. He will not let me pour the beer as I joggled the barrel once and he had to wait for a couple of hours to let it calm down before he could have a drink.

Once he was comfortably seated, with a cigarette in his hand, Douglas seemed a bit happier – about as cheerful as a hired mute at a bankrupt's funeral, who knows he won't be paid.

"I'm sorry, sir," Douglas began deferentially, "I didn't want to have to worry you at this time of night, but I just had to see you. It's about Stella's death. There's something about it which I can't quite understand. I've tried all ways of puzzling it out, but I can't see any explanation. I hope you can."

"Come on, son," the old man was gruffly encouraging, "take a pull at yer beer an' try to get yer story straight. Just try an' tell me exactly what ye mean as simply as ye can."

"Well," Douglas swallowed some of his beer and started again, "as you know, I was a bit drunk at the party and I lay down on the couch to sleep it off. It took me a bit of time sleeping it off and I suppose that when I woke I wasn't terribly bright. I offered to help Stella in the kitchen and I did so, peeling the mushrooms for her while she made the toast and did the cooking. It's about that I want to tell you. You see," his face was frank

87 Michael James Denham White's *Animal Cytology and Evolution* was first published in 1945.

and unhappy, "I had a little too much to drink again last night and it all came back to me."

He reached out and helped himself to another of my cigarettes, sorting out the ideas in his head before speaking.

"The kitchen in the house in Mecklenburgh Square is in the basement. Well, Stella and I went down there and started foraging around. We found the remains of the mushrooms she and Mary had brought from the country – Roger had asked them if he could give some to one of his friends, and we also found one of these little chip baskets of mushrooms – but not the mushrooms you get in the fields – the ones that people grow in cellars. Well, Stella looked at these and then said, 'Let's give the people upstairs the real mushrooms and eat the tasteless ones ourselves. What do you say?' I said I didn't mind, as I'm not what you'd call terribly fussy about food. So we peeled the country mushrooms first and started cooking them. While Stella was doing that part of the job, I peeled the cultivated ones. We, Stella and myself, must have eaten two or three minutes after the others. But you see what's worrying me, don't you? How did that Death Cap thing get in among the cultivated mushrooms?"

"Huh," the Professor grunted. His brows were creased in thought. "I'll admit it's an unlikely accident, but maybe the *Amanita* fell out o' the field mushrooms an' got mixed with the cultivated."

"No," Douglas was decisive, "that couldn't have happened. The shop mushrooms were covered with a piece of cellophane which I had to tear open before I could get at them."

"Then, maybe, the *Amanita* was left lying about and got included in the second lot."

Douglas shook his head. "That couldn't have happened. You see, as there are no maids in the house we all clean up together. So when I caught up with Stella I cleaned up the things that had been used, to save myself work later on. Stella had to use some of them again, but I'd have noticed if there was anything left lying about."

He drained his beer-mug and looked gloomily into the depths of it until the old man hoisted himself out of his chair and stumped over to the barrel to refill it.

"Well, sir," Douglas looked at the Professor expectantly, "can you give me any explanation of the presence of a poison toadstool among cultivated mushrooms? I, myself, cannot see how it would get there, can you?"

The old man lay back in his chair with his eyes half closed. He squinted along his cigar.

I felt pretty bewildered myself. I agreed with Douglas that it was very odd that a Death Cap should have managed to get into a sealed packet of mushrooms which had never been nearer the country than the smell of manure in a cellar.

"Umhum," the old man took his cigar out of his mouth and carefully dislodged a tottering inch of ash. "It certainly looks as though there was somethin' funny afoot. I can't say, Newsome, whether there really is anythin' fishy in yer story, but ye did quite right to come to me."

He leaned over to the low table beside him and untangled the telephone from the books and papers which seemed to have snowed upon it. The telephone is one of his favourite bugbears. It seems to him to be an invention of the devil, which he has to make use of by way of a penance for being born into the twentieth century.

After some palaver with the exchange and a considerable flow of soft abuse, the old man got through to Chief Inspector Bishop.

"Hey, you, Reggie," he growled into the mouthpiece, "I want you. Come on over." The Chief Inspector lives in Highgate[88] and the old man, who usually travels by car, has an idea that Highgate is just round the corner from our house. "I don't care if ye were just thinkin' of goin' to bed – it's still early an' I'll put ye up for the night if I keep ye late. I tell ye it's important. Dam' it, man," his voice was rather plaintive, "do I ever haul ye out on a wild goose chase, as ye call it? Well," his voice was slow as the Chief Inspector recited a long list of such occurrences, "these were kinda mistakes, before I got really goin' in me career as a detective. Tell me now, how many false alarms ha' there been in the last two years?"

The Chief Inspector gave up the struggle. He knows as well as I do that there's no point in struggling against the Professor when he has made up his mind. If the Chief Inspector had said he would not come over, either the old man would have kept on the telephone all night, or else he would have suddenly arrived at the Bishop's flat, which is a small and exquisite place, not at all suited to the Professor's hippopotamus-like behaviour.

The Professor, with the appearance of Perseus[89] after dealing with the

---

88 Highgate is a select suburb of London lying to the north-east of Hampstead Heath. Karl Marx (1818-1883) is buried in Highgate Cemetery.

89 Perseus was the legendary founder of Mycenae and the vanquisher of Medusa, one of the Gorgons.

Medusa, untangled the flex of the telephone from his person and laid it down.

"Well, son," he turned to Douglas, "I'm doin' the best I can for ye. The Chief Inspector'll hear what ye say an' will try an' make up his mind as to whether there's a case to go ahead on. I guess he'll begin by poo-pooin' the idea completely, an' then he'll complain that he's an overworked policeman, but finally he'll get around to lookin' into it. In the meantime, son, it might be kinda helpful if ye'd give me some sort o' account o' the inhabitants o' that house."

Douglas looked rather doubtful. "Well, you really should get hold of Arthur Loftus. He knows all about everyone. That's his speciality. He really is an actor. He was unfit for military service during the war so he got quite a few jobs. It was easy for any man to get a job in those days. In fact, a woman offered *me* a job in a rep. at Rugby and I had the hell of a job shaking her off. She thought that I was an actor because I was in the *Arts Theatre Club*, and when I said I wasn't she said that didn't matter as she could make me into one."

He laughed rather sadly as he thought of himself as an actor.

"However, I'll do my best about the household. First, of course, there's Roger. Everybody knows Roger. He's a decent sort and he has a little money and his great aunt Jemima or someone left him that house. He doesn't need a whole house and so he lets anyone who likes stay there. Nobody pays any rent, but when the rates come in Roger sticks a pin through them and leaves them stuck in the hall and we all put what we can towards them. Roger makes up what is short. The same happens with the phone and the gas and the electricity, though people do try and put money in a box for trunk and toll calls.[90] I have stayed there for quite a long time. Of course the population of the house is always shifting, but there are one or two people who, like myself, have been there for over a year."

He took a gulp of beer and that reminded me I was thirsty, so I up-ended my mug as a gesture to the Professor that it was empty. He did his duty as a host.

90 In the United Kingdom a trunk call was a long distance one which required an operator to make the connection and which, in the early days, had to be pre-booked. Toll calls, on the other hand, were local and could be connected by the operator while the caller waited. Subscriber Trunk Dialling (STD) was introduced in 1959 which meant that 18,000 subscribers in the Bristol area were able to make trunk calls without the aid of the operator.

"Take Harold Ironside, for instance," Douglas went on, "you know he was an all-in-wrestler before the war. Well during the war he was a sergeant instructor in the army till he got muscle-bound or something. When he came out he spent what money he had on going to an art school. He was quite bust when he met Roger, and Roger liked him and offered him a bed. Since then he has made a little money. He's not a good artist, but he turns out the sort of thing which some people like to keep standing on their mantelpieces – at least his stuff is better than the dreadful plaster nudes you get in the stores. I'm not sure that Roger is getting on with him very well at the moment. I think there was some trouble about Stella. It's funny. Until Max came along I thought it was Mary that was in love with Roger and, though I never thought he would marry, I thought he was more than ordinarily fond of her."

This was news to me. I knew of course that Mary addressed Roger as "darling", but then she addressed everyone in the same way. I had just thought it was the convention of the theatre. Whenever I go into the *Arts Theatre Club* I am almost snowed under with the meaningless shower of "darlings" and "dearests".

"Arthur Loftus," said Douglas, "now I don't like him. I think he's a nasty scaley pimp. The sort of thing you find under large stones in damp woods. You know – all pale and yellow from the lack of light. He more or less asked Roger if he could stay. The real thing I have against him is that even when he has money he never offers to pay a share of anything. Whenever any of the rest of us has any money he brings in some food or a bottle of booze or something for the good of the household. Now Arthur never does that. He's the sort of chap who may have a pound or two in his pockets, but if he sees that you have a pound or two as well he will try and borrow from you, as a matter of principle. I think he stinks. He knows too much about people's private lives and he is always making mischief. I think a lot of people are rather afraid of him."

I held out my packet of Player's and he took one. As he had spoken of Arthur Loftus I had seen that Douglas really was capable of not liking someone. I had always thought of him as a neutral sort of chap myself. The sort of fellow who just took people at their own valuation and left it there.

"Then there's Alec Dolittle. I don't think he's anything more than a drunken journalist and as randy as a rat. He doesn't do much work, and he's a frightful scrounger. On the other hand, when he has any money, while he won't pay his debts, he'll take everyone out and make them blind drunk. There's rather a funny story about him before the war. At that time he used to make a habit of borrowing people's typewriters, and then he would pop[91] them. I will say for him that he always gave the owner of the machine the ticket so that he could go and unpawn it, and he never pawned for more than two or three pounds. Well, there came a day when Alec had made a lot of money. I don't know whether he'd made a scoop or whether he had burgled it. Anyhow he went out and he bought himself a typewriter of his own. He still had quite a lot of money left so he decided that he'd go on the binge. When Alec goes on the binge he is apt to lose anything he has with him and he knows this, so for the sake of safety he dumped his typewriter in Leicester Square tube station[92] left luggage office and buzzed off round to a club in Long Acre to slake his thirst. That was the night the I.R.A.[93] left the bomb in the left luggage office and when Alec, who, having been blotto knew nothing about this, turned up in the morning for his typewriter, all they could give him was their regrets and a couple of spokes. It was really a bit tough, but on the other hand most of those who had lent him typewriters felt that it was almost a bit of divine justice."

The old man chortled at this story of Alec Dolittle's misfortunes. I must say that it did seem to me a fitting punishment for the popper of other men's typewriters, but all the same I felt rather sorry for Alec, who I quite liked, in spite of the touches for sundry five shillings which he used to apply fairly regularly.

"These," said Douglas, "are all the people who were in the house, staying, at the night of the party. Except of course Mary and Stella. I like both Mary and Stella. In fact," his pale face flushed a little, "I've had a thing about both of them at different times. As a matter of fact," he spoke rather quickly, "I had asked Stella to marry me that very night. Of course she said no." He remarked on this without any surprise or feeling. "It is quite obvious that I could never hope to keep a wife, and if I had one she would soon get tired of my ways. You see," he became confidential, "I am a bit erratic in my habits. That's why I like living in Roger's house. Nobody minds what I do, so long as I'm not sick when I'm drunk, and I'm *never*

91 'Pop' is a slang term for pawning.
92 Leicester Square tube station is located on Charing Cross Road.
93 The Irish Republican Army planted bombs that exploded at both the Leicester Square and Tottenham Court Road tube stations on the 3rd February 1939; fortunately there were no injuries or victims.

sick. To be quite honest I don't quite know why I asked Stella to marry me. I suppose it must have been because she was paying so much attention to Harold. Maybe I got a bit jealous, or something."

I thought that Stella must indeed have been a very much sought after young woman, what with Harold and Roger and, it now transpired, Douglas. I could see that she had been very beautiful and rather charming, but I wouldn't, myself, have given Mary for her and all the gold in the United States.

"Urrgh," the Professor suddenly grunted, "when ye were makin' the mushrooms on toast that night, can ye remember which o' the household came into the kitchen? That might be of help."

"Oh," Douglas was slightly vague, "so far as I can remember everyone looked in at one time or another. You see, Stella and I were the cooks, and the others came to carry various oddments upstairs. We didn't eat in the kitchen, of course, and so plates and knives and so on had to be taken up to Roger's room. Nearly everyone helps on these occasions. Mary came down with a drink for Stella and one for me. I can tell you that I needed it badly. Roger helped us to carry some of the food upstairs, so did Mary. Harold collected the cutlery. Arthur Loftus didn't help much. He just stood around with a glass in his hand, destroying people's reputations. And I don't think there was anything for Alec to do. He was slightly tight but full of good stories."

"Grrr," the old man growled. "I know what it is. Ye're all slightly fuddled an' ye can't remember exactly the way things happened. I get that way, meself, sometimes, son, so ye needn't think I'm criticisin' ye."

At that moment the electric bell rang piercingly. I got up and let Chief Inspector Bishop into the house. He is not a beer drinker, so, on the way back into the room, I collected a bottle of brandy and a glass.

CHAPTER SEVEN

FUSS AND BOTHER

AFTER DOUGLAS had left, the Professor peered at the Bishop from the gap between his bushy eyebrows and his steel-rimmed glasses.

"Well, Bishop," he boomed expectantly, "What d'ye think o' that? D'ye agree wi' me that there's a bit o' fishy business somewhere?"

The Chief Inspector rolled a sip of brandy round his mouth before he replied.

"No, John," he said, "to be perfectly honest I think that that young man has been imagining things. As you say, he was in love with the girl and I think his trouble is that he cannot believe that she is dead. He wants to justify her death and to be revenged on someone for it. He cannot beat up blind fate and so he tries to catch hold of some person who can be made to suffer for it. I think I can understand his point of view, even if I cannot quite see what he hopes to gain from it. Apart from anything else, old Mountjoy, for all his beastliness, is a good coroner and if there'd been the slightest suspicion of anything wrong he would have pounced on it. As you yourself noticed, he was definitely antagonistic. You know that he is a fervent anti-drink exponent or crank? Yes. Well he would have pounced on someone who is content to let things go the easy way. And in a case where the victim had refused to see a doctor until it was too late, he was especially vigilant."

"Ho, so you think that, d'ye?" the old man howled and his eyebrows bristled, "Did it never occur to ye that Mountjoy was so dam' concerned wi' the precious sanctity o' the thunderin' medical profession that he was payin' attention to that an' to nothin' else? The fact that it had bin a drinkin' party an' that no doctor was called was quite enough to distract his attention from everythin' else. I tell ye that the man's a dunderhead – he's got his blinkin' preconceived notions an' he won't let anythin' else into his block. Approach thin's in a spirit o' honest enquiry? Bah! He approaches thin's knowin' all an' unwillin' to admit that he knows nothin'. The man's a dam' public danger an' he ought to be put in a straight-jacket. Ye should tell him to go boil his head – the softenin' wouldn't do it any harm an' it might improve it."

"All the same, John," the Chief Inspector was insistent, "I must say that if I had been in Mountjoy's place my findings would have been exactly the same. If this young man Newsome had his suspicions, why didn't he voice them at the inquest? He was called in evidence and he had his chance. All he had to do was to mention the cultivated mushrooms and the matter would have been fully thrashed out then."

"Bah!" the old man was scornful, "It's easy to see, Reggie, that you never drink too much. If ye'd gi' yerself the chance, ye'd be able to understand what happened. Young Newsome had bin' drinkin' heavily an' he was wakened from his stupor an' set to work. I've no doubt but that he did his work in a mechanical way, wi'out the slightest attention to what he was doin'. Then he starts broodin' about the girl's death. While he's still broodin' he goes out an' gets drunk again. Then he sees all his actions quite plain. He knows exactly what he was doin' when he was still drunk the other night. Say someone in the pub opened somethin' wi' a cellophane wrapper – the sight o' that 'ud be quite sufficient to bring back the sight o' himself openin' the cellophane cover o' the punnet full o' cultivated mushrooms. Once he'd seen that the rest would come back to him plain, an' the boy'd ha' bin a fool, which he's not, if he'd let the matter rest there. Nobody in his senses is going to plant *Amanita* among cultivated mushrooms, which, mind ye, grow from cultivated spore, an' are not the same as the common field mushroom. The cultivated mushroom is the result o' intensive selection on the part o' the growers. Ye can see that the next time ye pass a greengrocer's shop – look at the cultivated mushrooms – they're all the same size. Look at a basket o' field mushrooms an' ye'll find that they're all sizes an' shapes. Ye see what I mean?"

The Chief Inspector was still doubtful.

"After all," he said slowly, "how do we know that the packaged mushrooms were cultivated? They might easily have been mushrooms from a field which had been selected for their perfect shape and put up in a cellophane wrapper."

"Yah," the old man was indignant, "what do we pay a police force to do for us? Ye couldn't try and find out could ye? It would be too much trouble, wouldn't it?"

"You forget," the Bishop was bland and unruffled, "that the police force has enough to do without running around after every brain-storm that comes your way, John. I am a busy man and my time is fully occupied in dealing with the cases that reach the police in the normal course of events. You can't expect me to go out looking for cases, to give myself more work, particularly when these cases have been satisfactorily dealt with already by the proper authorities. In this case the proper authority was the coroner's court, and you may remember that I was present at that, and I must say that the whole affair seemed to me to be a pure case of accidental poisoning."

"Phooey," said the Professor with the air of one who has had a bright idea, "If the thunderin' *Amanita* had bin cooked wi' the rest o' the mushrooms ye'd ha' expected some o' the others to ha' bin ill, wouldn't ye? The dam' thing 'ud ha' distilled its blinkin' poison through the whole dish, wouldn't it? An' who was ill? Nary a one. Even if it had bin in the cultivated mushrooms, young Newsome 'ud ha' eaten some, and did he look sick? No. I tell ye that the more I think of it the more I become convinced that Newsome is right an' that there was some kinda jiggery pokery wi' the mushrooms."

"Yes," the Bishop weighed the idea in his mind, "you may have something there. I would need to know more about the subject of mushroom poisoning before I could give you an opinion on the subject. But you must understand that it is very difficult for me to take any official action on the word of a young man who was admittedly drunk at the time of the occurrence. I'll tell you this, however, John. If it had been anyone else than you who had come to me with this story, I would have turned it down straight. On the other hand, you have been known to be right about the most unusual things, so I am willing to make a few unofficial enquiries, just to satisfy myself that you are wrong."

Professor Stubbs blew out his checks triumphantly. He beamed at the well-fed and comfortable Chief Inspector and he turned to me.

"There, Max," he said with the gloat hardly disguised in his voice, "I told you he would listen to sense. He's a well brought up little boy an' he respects the opinions o' his elders."

This pat on the top of the head seemed to bring the Bishop no pleasure.

"All right, John," he said, "all right. There's no need for you to plume yourself[94] on your persuasiveness. I would just like to know what it is you want me to find out."

94 i.e. congratulate yourself.

"Well." the Professor was thoughtful, "I suppose ye'd better find where the mushrooms were bought an' whether they were, indeed, the cultivated sort. Once ye've found that out, ye'll begin to know where ye are."

I took a long pull at my beer. I was not happy. It seemed to me that I had once more wandered into a murder case. And I must admit that I do not like murders occurring among my friends. The Chief Inspector seemed to read my thoughts.

"As for you, Max," he said severely, "I grow more and more convinced that you ought to be shut up as a public danger. Death seems to follow you around like your shadow."

He was right. I felt most uncomfortable. I take the Professor out for an evening on the booze and someone chooses to shoot a commando knife into another chap's back.[95] I go out to buy some books and I find two men lying dead in a gas-filled room.[96] Now I go out to a party with some friends and a member of the household dies of Death Cap poisoning.

All this could hardly have been expected to add to my peace of mind, but the major thing about it all was that I felt quite convinced that Douglas was right, and that Stella Mortimer had been poisoned by someone who had meant to bring about her death.

Thinking back over what I knew of Stella, I found that it did not add up to much. She had been very beautiful, with green eyes and red hair. She had always been absolutely charming to me, and, so far as I could judge, to everyone else she knew.

I remember being annoyed with Arthur Loftus one day. I had said something about Mary as an actress and he had looked at me with that odd fishlike look which he sometimes affected.

"My dear," he had said, with stress on the 'dear', "Stella Mortimer can act Mary off a stage any time she wants to. If I was Mary I would pray that fate kept me off the same stage."

"What do you know about acting?" I asked rudely, "I notice that you seem to spend most of your time 'resting'."

The taunt had not worried him. He had merely smiled mysteriously, and, I guessed, gone away to tell someone that that tall and ugly botanist,

95 See *Take Thee a Sharp Knife*, published by John Westhouse in 1946, and re-printed by Lomax Press in 2012.
96 See *Bodies in a Bookshop*, published by John Westhouse in 1946, and reprinted by Dover in 1984.

Boyle, had "the most frightful thing" about Mary.

Stella, I remembered Mary saying, was of a very independent turn of mind. She had disapproved of her mother's American marriage and had not had any correspondence with her since. I knew little about her morals. I am no moralist and such things do not really interest me. If she wanted to sleep with people that was her business. Arthur would most certainly have been able to give the police an almost complete list of any such people.

"By the way, Bishop," I addressed the Chief Inspector, "if you want to lay your hands on all the gossip about what went on in that house, you'd better contact a young man called Arthur Loftus. He is a semi-professional minder of other people's business. I don't like him and I don't know anyone who does, but he can tell you all about people. He is a sort of fly-paper gossip."

The Chief Inspector made a note in his pocket-book. He looked very tired. I knew that look of old. It meant that he was sorting things out in his mind. It was one of his deceptive disguises which took in a lot of people when they first met him. They thought that such a sleepy and plump person could not be really astute. They sometimes found out, to their disadvantage, how very wrong they were.

The Professor looked as though he was set for an all night session. This means that whether he knows everything or nothing about a case he will settle down and put up problematical cases as Aunt Sallies,[97] which he will then proceed to demolish as fast as he can. I have never been able to decide on the value of such a game myself, but Professor Stubbs claims that it clears the brain.

From the look in the Chief Inspector's eye I could see that he also knew what was in the old man's mind. Like myself, the Chief Inspector likes to have a good ration of sleep, and, again like myself, he does not see any reason for the Professor's Aunt Sally performances.

The old man opened his mouth but before he could speak, the Bishop interposed firmly.

"No, no, John," he said, "I'm not going to sit here all night to listen to you putting up cases against people of whom I know next to nothing. I am a hard working public servant and if I do not get my sleep, my work suffers and then the public suffers. You would not like me to have that on my conscience, would you?"

---

97 An Aunt Sally was a fairground game in which the contestants attempted to knock a clay pipe out of the mouth of a figurine old woman.

"I just thought o' one or two little points," the old man pleaded, "an' I thought I might kinda get them clear in me head by discussin' them for a few minutes. Not that I mean to go on all night." His voice expressed his surprise at such a thought. "Will you not just stop an' hear what I got to say? It'll only take a few minutes."

The Chief Inspector shook his head decisively. "No, John, I will not stop to hear what you have to say. I know your 'few minutes'. They are liable to last till breakfast time."

He got up and picked up his overcoat from its resting place on top of a pile of books. He said good-night in a voice that said that he meant it, and went out into the dark.

When I got back into the room I found that the Professor had refilled our mugs. I saw that I was for it. I determined that I would only stay till I had finished my pint.

"Now," he said argumentatively, "let's see what we got. Here we ha' a young girl, beautiful an' cheerful, who has apparently bin murdered for no reason at all. At least we'll take it that it is a murder an' not just a common accident. Now who o' the people in the case 'ud ha' wanted to murder her. Let's begin wi' yer girl friend. Can ye think o' any reason why she might ha' wished to kill Stella Mortimer?"

I was, not unnaturally, pretty indignant, and I made my feelings clear. I pointed out that Mary and Stella were friends, great friends, and I also made it clear that I would as soon suspect myself as Mary. I might just as well have spent my time addressing a brick wall. I'd probably have got more satisfaction out of the echo. The Professor just went straight ahead, as if I had not spoken.

"Well, o' course," he rumbled along, "there's the possibility that she wanted Roger Sharon for herself an' could see no reason why he had preferred Stella. She might ha' wanted him badly enough for that."

I spluttered and protested. I thought the old man was really going a bit too far.

"Umm," he said, lending the sixty-fourth of an ear to my voice, "we'll need to look into her. Next in the list comes young Newsome. At the moment it looks as though we could acquit him. The case was properly closed an' there was no need for him to bother about re-openin' it. Unless, o' course, he realised that he had made some sort o' blunder an' was tryin' to forestall possible suspicion by gettin' his word in ahead o' the others. Um, though, I don't think that idea'll hold water. He's clever enough, but not as dam' clever as that. What d'ye think, Max?"

"I certainly don't think that you can suspect Douglas. As you say the case was finished with and it would have remained so, but for the fact that he came out of his drunken loss of memory and remembered his actions. He might never have remembered them, or claimed that he never remembered them. After all, if you think of the situation inside that house, you'll realise that nobody in it would give a second thought to the absence of a punnet of mushrooms. They'd just suppose that someone had been hungry and had used them. Oh," an idea suddenly struck me, "I now know why Stella looked so surprised when I suggested to her that she might be suffering from fungus poisoning. She knew – and she was the only person beside Douglas who did know – that she had eaten the cultivated mushrooms and not those that she and Mary had gathered in the country. She knew that, and so she could hardly believe that she was likely to have been poisoned by a cultivated mushroom, even if she had made a mistake in picking the others. Of course she was very weak at the time, for she had been very ill, and I suppose she thought of the matter for a moment and then dismissed it from her mind, assuming that if she was suffering from poisoning, there must have been one or two of the field mushrooms in the dish she ate. After all it was Douglas who cleared up while she was cooking and who was positive that *all* the field mushrooms had been used before he started on his and her meal. She was probably pretty busy with a pan and would not have time to notice a little thing like whether Douglas had popped one or two left-overs in with their share. Douglas was quite certain. I think he probably has one of these photographic memories[98] when he is tight. He would have a mental picture of the table being perfectly clear of all pieces of mushroom, just before he started on the second lot of peeling."

"Um, yes" the old man growled, "ye've certainly got a point there. Whoever did the job was certainly bein' pretty clever. There were only two people who could have remembered what went on in the kitchen, an' one o' them's dead an' t'other was drunk."

I could see exactly what he meant. After all, how was anyone in that house to know that there were cultivated as well as field mushrooms in the house? Speaking from a purely impersonal point of view I could see that the murderer had had damned bad luck.

98 Todd also had a photographic memory.

The old man was showing signs of continuing. I followed the example of the Bishop, and, despite his protests, rose and went to bed.

CHAPTER EIGHT

THE MOTH AND THE STAR[99]

WHEN I rose in the morning I could hear the sound of bustling below me. A voice was raised in what might have passed for song. The old man was bellowing out some music hall song of his youth. This was a damned bad sign. It meant that he was on the warpath. It meant that no botanical work to speak of would be done for quite a time. It meant, in fact, that I was in for a bad few days until the case had been cleared up.

My temper was not improved by the fact that I had to use a new blade in my razor. I have never mastered the art of shaving with a new blade and I always cut my face. This morning I cut it rather worse than usual. So I was in a thoroughly vile frame of mind when I went downstairs.

The Professor was bustling about as if he had not a care in the world. He was watering plants with the gay abandon of a musical comedy star doing a sort of garden dance.

He was already dressed in his wrinkled grey suit. When he gets dressed before breakfast I feel doubly depressed. I wished to God I'd gone away on holiday.

The only cheering thing was a note from Mary. It was affectionate enough to almost offset my depression. She suggested that I should go down to Linton and stay the night, since she could not get up to town. She gave me her phone number, which I had forgotten to ask for. I don't know why it had escaped my memory, but I'd had so much else to think about – principally her presence beside me – that I had forgotten it.

Professor Stubbs looked at me across the toast and coffee. I could see

99 *The Moth and the Star* is the title of a fable by James Thurber published in *Fables of Our Time* in 1940. The moral of the story is "Who flies afar from the sphere of our sorrow is here today and here tomorrow." Todd knew James Thurber and had met him in London during the 1930s.

that he was rubbing his mental hands together with glee. I myself like a quiet life, but there's nothing the old man likes so well as disorganisation. He likes having everything in a mess around him. It seems that he can order things in his brain under these circumstances. So far as I'm concerned most of his organisation disorganises me. I don't like murders. I had enough battle, murder, and sudden death[100] during the war to do me for the rest of my days. In fact, so far as I'm concerned I want nothing more than a little peace and plenty of quiet, so that I'll be able to sit down and do my work without needing to worry how I'm going to pay the rent or what I'll eat tomorrow or the day after.

Life with Professor Stubbs could not be described as restful, even by the most hopeful person. Either I'm sweating my guts out on some subject connected with botany (and I don't mind that in the least; that is my job), or else I'm tearing around trying to keep the old man out of trouble because he has got on the scent of murder. It sometimes seems to me that I've had nothing but trouble ever since I became his assistant. One of these days, I told myself, you'll get your holiday, and, by God, it will be some holiday. No murders, no trouble. I will wander around the countryside finding plants, just for the fun of it.

Rather to my surprise the old man opened up the conversation with a discourse on the failings of most professional botanists. I began to cheer up a little. This didn't sound like the usual hunting call. It sounded more like the normal call to work.

Of course, I hadn't realised that this *was* in fact a botanical murder. The old man soon got round to the subject of fungi, and I realised I was in for it.

When I got a chance to put in a word for myself I announced, "Oh, by the way, sir, I'm afraid I'll be going away tomorrow for a couple of days. I hope you don't mind."

He looked at me suspiciously, as if I was holding something back from him.

"Eh?" he growled, "Where'r ye goin'? Nowhere too far away, I hope, for I may be needing ye."

"Oh" I replied, "I've just had an invitation from a friend to go down and stay for a couple of nights and I thought I might as well take advantage of it."

"What part o' the country are ye goin' to?" he asked, unabashed by my

---

100 Leslie Charteris used this phrase in *The Saint Closes the Case* in 1930 to summarise the Saint's attitude to life.

obvious unwillingness to be communicative.

"If you really want to know," I was insulting, "I'm going to Essex. What do you want to know for?"

He beamed at me in a friendly manner. I thought he had something up his sleeve so I prepared to be on the defensive.

"Humm," he mumbled reflectively, "Ye wouldn't by any chance to be goin' to see yer girl, Mary what's her name? If ye were goin' there I'd take it as an obligement if ye'd gather me a few mushrooms, and you can include any *Amanita* that ye find."

"All right, all right," I snarled at him, "I'll bring you your *Amanita*, and I'll ask Mrs. Farley to serve it up to you by way of a savoury, and I hope you enjoy it."

It was not a propitious beginning to a morning's work. I tried to settle down to doing one or two things of my own as I knew that the old man, as usual, would potter around the house in the most annoying way, upsetting all my order in the books by pulling them out of one place and putting them into others after reading a paragraph or two.

Half-way through the morning he came and looked over my shoulder and read what I was writing. He pointed out one or two statements in my notes about which he felt dubious. The awful thing was that on looking at them again I could see he was right. This did not improve my temper. He looked at me in a half apologetic way.

"I was wonderin', Max," his voice was not too sure of itself, "if ye'd like to come out for a drink."

Well, I thought to myself, anything is better than this state of hardly subdued irritation. I said I thought it would be a good idea to go out and have a drink.

It wasn't until we were held up by some traffic lights in Mornington Crescent[101] that I realised that the offer of a drink was not without its purpose.

The Professor leaned towards me and made himself heard above the noise of the engine, which sounded as though all the horse-power in the world was straining to get loose beneath the bonnet.

101 Mornington Crescent was built in the 1820s as a development of 36 town-houses and was named after the Earl of Mornington, the Duke of Wellington's brother. Dickens attended a school in the crescent, which lies on the south edge of Camden.

"Where," he enquired noisily, "d'y'r friends drink lunch time? I was thinkin' we might drop in an' have a pint along o''em."

I scowled, but I gave it up. There was no future in opposing the Professor when he was like that. I felt like an Austin Seven[102] trying conclusions with a bull-dozer.

"All right," I said wearily, almost as wearily as the Bishop, "You win. Let's go to *The Lamb*[103] in Lamb's Conduit Street.[104] I expect we'll find one or two of them there."

Rather to the surprise of a policeman, who had the good sense to say nothing, the Professor changed course and the car shot away down to the right. I was afraid the old man was going to knock a bit off the *Unity Theatre*[105] as we went round Goldington Square, but he negotiated that difficulty all right. We finally made *The Lamb* without a scratch and with only slight damage to my nerves.

Inside *The Lamb* I saw Roger sitting with Harold. There was something the matter with Roger's face. His lips were rather puffy and his right eye looked as though it had been banged on something. It was half closed and there was a bluish yellow look about the swollen skin. Then I realised that Harold had a long strip of pink sticking plaster along one side of his chin.

"Hullo," said Roger cheerfully. I hadn't seen him looking so cheerful for several days, not since before his party at any rate. "What are you two drinking?"

We had pints. There was something here that I could not quite understand. The last time I had seen Roger and Harold they had been ready to fly at one another's throats and they would gladly have battered one another insensible, but here they were, looking as though there had never been anything between them.

---

102 The Austin Seven was a small economy car produced by the Austin Motor Company of Longbridge from 1922 to 1939.

103 *The Lamb* was built in the 1720s and refurbished in the Victorian era. It incorporates one of the few remaining examples of snob screens which prevented a well-to-do drinker from being seen by his social inferiors (and vice versa).

104 Lamb's Conduit Street runs north to south from Guilford Street to Theobald's Road. It is named after William Lamb who built a conduit in 1577 to carry water along two thousand yards of lead piping from a spring of drinking water at his own expense (£1,500).

105 The *Unity Theatre* started its life in 1936 in Britannia Street, but by 1937 had moved to Goldington Street (rather than Square, which did not exist).

I tried to keep my eyes off Roger's face, but I'm afraid he noticed my effort.

"Oh," he said, without embarrassment, "You're looking at my face. Well I suppose I'd better tell you before you get the story out of Arthur Loftus. He was there at the time and his story is sure to be too vivid for my liking. Don't you think it would come better from us, Harold old man?"

"He should be shot," Harold spoke slowly, "mischief making little bastard. I don't often like to think about the army, but I would like to have had him in my squad for a few days. By God, I'd have made him sweat."

"Oh, well," Roger was tolerant, "I suppose he can't help himself. He just was made that way. Anyhow, last night I'd had a drop too much to drink."

"So had I," interposed Harold, looking slightly ashamed of himself.

"And," Roger went on, "I'm afraid I got rather irritated with Harold and I swung at him with a bottle. Damnable thing to do but I suppose in my drunken condition I knew I hadn't a chance with my fists."

"Not at all," Harold was not perturbed, "you just hit me with what you had in your hands. You didn't stop to lay it down. I can't say that I blame you. After all, I do look pretty big."

"Harold didn't bother to hit me back," Roger's voice was rather ashamed, "He just grabbed me and held me till I came to my senses. I did all this," he gestured towards his face, "in trying to struggle free from him. He picked me up as if I had been a baby and laid me on the couch, holding me there till I calmed down."

"Aw," Harold was mildly bashful, "forget it. It was all a misunderstanding. It wasn't your fault and it wasn't altogether mine. If he wasn't such a filthy little weed I'd take a swing at Arthur. But it doesn't matter now, does it, Roger?"

I was still slightly in the dark about what had caused all the trouble. I knew there had been some jealousy about Stella but I could not sort it out. It had seemed to me that things had been cleared up when Mary had rather tactlessly announced that Roger had proposed to Stella.

"Bung ho!" the Professor tilted his glass and the pint disappeared, to join more pints than I liked to think about. He looked at Roger and Harold thoughtfully.

"Ha' ye seen young Newsome this mornin'?" he asked slowly.

Both Harold and Roger shook their heads. "No," the latter replied, "He came in very late last night and I haven't seen him at all today. Why?"

"Umm," the Professor seemed to be wondering what he should say next, "umm, well, ye see he came visitin' me last night wi' a load o' worry on his mind, an' I'm afraid I couldn't clear it up for him."

Slowly, and painstakingly, with the air of one explaining the first principles of biology to a group of very raw students, the old man outlined the story which Douglas had told us, stilling interruptions with an upraised hand. If I had been asked to put Douglas's story into a brief and connected narrative I could not have done it so well. The Professor had managed to get hold of all the salient points and he had organised them into a connected and telling whole.

"But, sir," Harold was the first to speak, "Douglas was drunk. He must have imagined the whole thing. After all, who would have wanted to hurt Stella? Of course," his voice was thoughtful, "I might have wanted to do in Roger or Roger might have wanted to bump me off, but I don't think either of us would have chosen that method."

"Thank you, Harold," replied Roger in a voice that did not sound very thankful. "I'm afraid, though, that Douglas wasn't as drunk as all that. You see there was a chip-basket full of cultivated mushrooms in the kitchen. I had bought it myself before I knew that Mary and Stella were bringing some up with them from the country. I never gave it another thought. I suppose I assumed that Stella in cooking had just mixed the two lots, hers and mine, together and that we'd all had some of both. I don't think I even mentioned the ones I'd bought to anyone at all. It never occurred to me to do so. You see you don't get poison toadstools in baskets of mushrooms bought in a shop. I have just been saying that it was a horrible and unhappy accident. I'm afraid, Max," he turned towards me, "that to some extent I've been blaming Mary for it. Stella knew mushrooms. She used to eat all sorts of fungi, and I knew that she would never make a mistake in picking them. When she was at school, she told me, they had a mistress who was very keen on these sort of things and who taught them all about them. I remember Stella bringing up some horrible looking flat red fungus one day – she called it a vegetable beefsteak. When I said I was sure it must be poison she said, 'Oh, no. I never pick any fungus that could be confused with a poison one – that's the only way to be safe.' And I must say that her vegetable beefsteak tasted all right – rather like aubergine. She wouldn't have made a mistake like that."

"Oh that's all right," I said rather uncomfortably, "even if it was Mary's fault it was an accident, but after what Douglas said last night, it doesn't look as though it was anyone's mistake. It looks as though it had been intentional."

"But," Roger went on, "as Harold says I don't see who could have wanted to kill Stella."

"No," Harold came to his support, "there are plenty of other people who might have been murdered. Take Arthur Loftus, for instance, I could think of dozens of people who would be glad to see the last of him. He's rather like the Poles in the story of Wyndham Lewis,[106] who, after the First World War, settled in a house and could not be got out of it. Roger invited him to stay for a week or two until he got a job."

"I didn't exactly invite him," Roger interposed, "He asked me if I could put him up for a few days, and naturally, not having anything tangible against him, I told him to come along."

"Well," said Harold, "he came along and he's settled in. He is a beastly drone. He never helps in anything and he takes from everyone. I must admit," his voice was rather defensive, "that there are times when none of us has any money and then, I'm afraid, we all have to scrounge on Roger, but when we do have money we try and make it up. Arthur gets money sometimes. He does odd jobs for the B.B.C., but when he has money we don't, as a rule, see him, or if we see him he never admits to having any money."

"Speak of the devil," I said with startling originality. The pale face of Arthur Loftus had peered round the door of the pub. He saw us and came over. There was one of these uncomfortable silences which occur when people have been talking about another person who suddenly appears.

"Hullo, hullo, hullo," said Arthur as he looked round at us, "a real gathering of the clans, what? Why the silence? Were you talking about me? If you were, please go on. There's nothing I like better than being talked about. It is all publicity."

"Hmm," the Professor was vaguely amused, "Maybe, Mr. Loftus, ye wouldn't like to hear what we were sayin' about ye. Maybe ye'd feel embarrassed by the flow o' high soundin' praise."

Arthur peered up at the bulk of the old man. His pale face winced. His eyes, I noticed were blue – the cloudy blue of a dead herring on a fishmonger's slab.

"I don't mind," he said, "what you were saying about me. It is better to

---

106 Todd knew Lewis and had visited him at his home in Notting Hill Gate a few times.

be talked about, even in disparagement, than not to be talked about at all. How's the face, Roger?"

"My face, Arthur," Roger was mildly stiff, "is my own business and it is quite well."

The girl behind the bar was waiting for Arthur to order a drink. He looked round at us all, saw that our mugs were full and said, in a pleased way, "Cheap round, what? I'll have a half of bitter."

Professor Stubbs, with brazen effrontery, put his mug to his lips and the beer drained away into nothingness.

"Since ye offer me a drink" he said breezily, "I'll ha' another pint o' bitter. Thank'ee kindly."

He slid the mug across the counter. Arthur risked the suspicion of a scowl. Harold and Roger were frankly amused. I hadn't thought of the trick, but I made haste to finish my pint.

"Thanks," I said, laying my mug beside the Professor's. The other two tumbled to the trick and did likewise. Arthur was not pleased. He finished his half-pint before we had done with our pints and stood waiting for someone to offer to buy him a round.

I was waiting to see what the old man would do next. He drained his beer, and looked round at Harold and Roger.

"Are ye ready?" he asked, and when they nodded, to Arthur's great surprise and undisguised disgust, he made for the door of the pub.

We followed him. Arthur stood for a moment waiting to see what he should do. He hesitated just a second too long. By the time he came to the door, the old man had the Bentley roaring and we all piled in. We drove down Lamb's Conduit Street, down Red Lion Street,[107] along Holborn[108] and then along Theobald's Road.[109] When the Bentley was halted by the red lights at the entrance to Lamb's Conduit Street again, the Professor leaned towards Roger.

107 Red Lion Street, which runs south from Theobald's Road to High Holborn, is named after Red Lyon Fields which was a location for duels in the 17th century.

108 Holborn is a district of London that historically stood just outside the old City of London.

109 Theobald's Road is named after King James I's hunting estate in Hertfordshire and runs west to east past Gray's Inn. During the period of Todd's story, locals pronounced it in a Shakespearean manner - Tibbult's Road - and Todd himself refers to this fact.

"Where'd ye buy these mushrooms?" he demanded, and Roger gestured up the street.

We stopped outside a little vegetable shop and got out of the car. A small woman with brightly hennaed hair came bustling forward.

"Good morning, Mr. Sharon," she said in a subdued voice, "that was a terrible accident that happened to your friend. And her so young and pretty too. Ah, well, the ways of the Lord are mysterious."

Roger did not like this much and I can't say that I blame him. He stood tongue-tied.

The old man stepped into the breach. "Ha' ye any mushrooms?" he asked.

The woman looked at him pityingly. Just beside her there was a display of small baskets of mushrooms, each of them covered neatly with cellophane. There was green lettering printed on the cellophane. The Professor bought a basket. We climbed back into the car.

He showed the basket to Roger. "Were the ones ye bought," he asked, "just the same as these, eh?"

Roger took them. He looked at the cellophane and shuddered slightly. "I don't think I'll ever want to eat a mushroom again as long as I live." Harold nodded his head. "Yes, so far as I can see they are just the same."

The name on the label and the address made it quite clear that the mushrooms were, in fact, cultivated ones. There was no chance that they were carefully selected and washed field mushrooms. If Douglas's story was to be believed, and I could see no reason why it should not be, there was indeed something very odd about Stella's death.

CHAPTER NINE

BEAUTY IS BUT A FLOWER

WHEN I got out of the little train – a little engine that seemed to date from the early eighteen-eighties had pulled it, puffing steam from every joint – Mary was standing on the platform to greet me.

My heart leapt at the sight of her and I felt about seventeen.

"Hullo, darling," she said, "it *was* nice of you to come. I've fixed up a room for you at *The Ravaging Boar*."

We walked up through the little town. Mary pointed out the repertory theatre. It was a tall, black weather-board building which looked as though it had once been one of these immense Essex barns. I asked Mary about it, and found that my guess was right. It had been turned into a theatre at considerable cost and with considerable difficulty, as it all had to be lined with asbestos boarding to make certain that there was no danger of fire.

It was dusk and the little town looked very pleasant in the twilight. At least, I told myself, you are in for a couple of quiet days. My room at *The Ravaging Boar* was extremely pleasant and there was a large log fire burning in the cosy little bar. Mary and I sat down to have a drink.

I did not say anything about Douglas's story. I thought that as I was to spend a couple of quiet nights I might just as well spend them free of all thoughts of murder.

Before we had time to finish our first drink the bar was invaded by a crowd of people. They all seemed to know Mary, and they all addressed her in the most affectionate terms. I had forgotten that I was coming down to Linton to stay with an actress. This meant, in a small town, that she was known to nearly everyone, and that, of course, my evenings would be broken by her performances. I felt my spirits rather damped by this, but then it could not be helped.

I was introduced to two girls, both of them rather masculine in appearance. They were sisters and ran the theatre. It was, apparently, their own property.

The trouble was that, with the influx of people from the theatre, the conversation became at once theatrical. I felt put out. However, there was no help for it, so I joined in the conversation as well as I could, picking up such threads as I knew about. It was rather like making lace with too few spools.

I was escorted along to the theatre by Mary and several friends. Mary had booked a seat for me. I thought I was to be left there, but not a bit of it. I was shown where my seat was and was then led into the back of the theatre. I was dumped in a room, called for some unknown reason the 'green' room, although the only green thing about it was a broken down sofa upon which I sat, swinging up and down on a broken leg as I breathed. This room was full of people in various stages of make-up. One young man was playing a gramophone in one corner. He put on a record of Fats Waller – *I'm Gonna Sit Right Down an' Write Myself a Letter*.[110] This was fine, but it rather clashed with a record of the Bach *Chaconne*[111] which drifted through from one of the dressing rooms, and, finally, a few minutes before the curtain rose, there was a further dissonance in the shape of *The Gondoliers*,[112] played loudly for the benefit, or otherwise, of the audience.

I removed myself from the green room, where I felt out of place and lost and finally found my way to my seat. Before I went I got a glimpse of Mary, her face covered thickly with white grease-paint. She did not look as charming as usual with this disguise.

"Come down after the show, darling," she said, "and have a cup of tea. I think we'll be in time to get a drink at *The Boar* after I've changed."

The play was not a very good play. It had all the loose ends and flat passages of a beginner's effort. It dealt with Joan of Arc. Mary was Joan.

Watching her act I felt the blood flow hotly through me. When she walked across the little stage, her movement had all the dignity of all the tragic queens of history. My heart nearly burst with the overflow of love. I remembered what Arthur Loftus had said about Stella as an actress and

---

110 *I'm Gonna Sit Right Down an' Write Myself a Letter* was written by Fred Ahlert and Joe Young and recorded by Fats Waller in 1935.

111 The final movement of Bach's *Partita for Violin No. 2*.

112 Also known as the *King of Barataria*, this Savoy opera was written by Gilbert and Sullivan and was first performed in 1889.

thought that if, indeed, she was better than Mary, she must have been very, very good.

Thinking of Stella I remembered a snatch from a poem by the Elizabethan, Thomas Nashe. The thought of it almost made me sick with sorrow.

Beauty is but a flower
Which wrinkles will devour:
Brightness falls from the air;
Queens have died young and fair;
Dust both closed Helen's eye.[113]

I could have sat there for hours, watching Mary in her progress to that final scene, and listening to her voice making something real out of the trivial and often too well-worn words of the incompetent playwright.

When the play finished and I wandered round to the green room again I was still subdued.

"Hello, darling," said Mary cheerfully. She was wiping grease-paint off her face. "How did you like it?"

"My God," I said, "I thought you were wonderful. Far too good for the play."

"It's not very good," she said, "is it? But you thought I was all right?"

I assured her that I thought she was far better then merely "all right." She went to finish changing and I sat on the edge of the sofa. A curious young man, who had played the Dauphin, came over and sat beside me. He had a face like a faun. This sounds like a cliché, but the fact is that his face was exactly like that of a faun. He even seemed to have pointed ears, and his short hair curled exactly like that of a classical faun. I wondered vaguely what kind of feet were hidden by his shoes. Mary had introduced us vaguely before the show. His name was Eric Owen. I noticed that, to complete the faun-like appearance, the corners of his eyes were slightly lifted towards the temples.

"Did you know Stella Mortimer?" he asked me suddenly.

"Only slightly," I replied. "Why?"

"Oh, she was to come down here," he replied, "She was unlucky. I can't understand how she came to make a mistake like that, can you?"

I wondered what he was fishing for. I was sternly determined not to say anything about Douglas's story. I changed the subject.

---

113 From Thomas Nashe's (1567-1601) *A Litany in Time of Plague.*

"Do you like it down here?" I asked. "Don't you find it terribly difficult to get up and down from town?"

"Oh, I don't mind it here much, and anyhow I won't be staying much longer. I'm leaving next week."

I didn't know whether I should commiserate with him or not. He went on.

"The trouble is I can't stand the Ugly Sisters. I always feel as though I'm playing Cinderella in their pantomime. Anyhow I've got a much better job in town. Arthur Loftus is coming here to take my place in the company."

"Oh," I was surprised. I had thought that Arthur had made up his mind not to work again, so long as Roger was willing to keep him in idleness. He had seemed to me to make enough pocket money out of the B.B.C. and borrowing to keep him going without real work.

"Why do you say 'Oh'?" the faun enquired, "Do you know him?"

"Only slightly," I replied again. I felt as thought I was being put through the third degree. The faun looked at me enquiringly.

"You work with Professor Stubbs, don't you?" he said, and I nodded my head. He lit a cigarette carefully, offering me one at the same time. He seemed to be wondering how to begin. It seemed to me that it was up to me to continue the conversation.

"Why do you ask?" I queried, setting my question as a kind of bait. He puffed at his cigarette and the blue smoke curled round his head.

He seemed to come to a decision.

"It was nothing," he said slowly, "only Arthur was down here for a day to fix things up at the same time that Stella was down. He tacked himself on to the two girls when they went mushroom picking. He did not stay with them for long, but came back saying that such a lot of stooping was not in his line. I just wondered whether he made a mistake in the few mushrooms that he picked. You know he loathed Stella."

Having got rid of this the faun rose to his feet and left the room. I was left to wonder what he had meant by his statement. Before I had time to get things straight in my mind Mary came back. The grease-paint had vanished and she looked like the Mary I knew. I said as much.

We wandered back to *The Boar* and found the bar full of people who were enjoying a last drink or two before closing time. The faun was there. I bought him a drink and, when Mary had left us alone for a moment, said, "What did you mean by your remarks about Arthur Loftus?"

"Oh, nothing, nothing," he replied, "It was just an idea that had occurred to me. It doesn't mean anything. I wouldn't like you to think that I meant anything by my remarks. Put it down to spite if you like. I liked Stella a lot, the hell of a lot," his voice was reflective and it turned bitter as he went on, "but I can't stand the sight, sound or name of Arthur Loftus. I would like to see him getting into trouble. I would like to make the little horror squirm. So you see, I'm afraid I was just being spiteful. I didn't mean anything really."

Mary returned and he bought a round, the last of the evening. I saw Mary back to her digs. We said good-night and she asked me to call round about ten the next morning, to have a cup of coffee. I walked slowly back to the hotel, my thoughts a jumble of my love for Mary and of what Eric Owen had said.

It was a fine morning and my spirits were high as I left the hotel. I had decided to shelve the problem raised by the faun until I got back to town. Mary was up and was wearing her blue silk dressing gown when I arrived. She was staying above a grocer's shop, in a small oak beamed room. The room looked very comfortable, and I saw that the grocer had provided her with a gas ring. We chatted about trivial things while she made the coffee.

"Where the hell's the milk pan got to?" she demanded from the depths which gave no answer. I pointed out a small aluminium pan, but that was not the right one – it always burned the milk. Finally she ran it to earth. It had fallen down behind a pile of *Theatre Arts Monthly*.[114] I began to think that she lived in almost as great a chaos as I did with the Professor. I looked along her bookshelves. There were the usual collection of French's acting editions, with things like *The Oxford Book of Sixteenth Century Verse*,[115] one or two Modern Library Giants[116] of *Modern American Plays*,[117] some odd

114 *Theatre Arts Monthly* was founded by Sheldon Cheney in 1916 and was published in Detroit by the Arts and Crafts Society. It merged with *The Stage* in 1948 and ceased publication in 1964.

115 *The Oxford Book of Sixteenth Century Verse*, was compiled by E.K. Chambers and was first published in 1932.

116 The Modern Library series was started in 1917 by Albert Boni and Horace Liveright, and contained over 1000 titles, mainly reprints, by the time it was brought to a close in 1970. The 'Giants' were first introduced as a sub-series in 1931.

117 There is no Modern Library edition with this title, 'Giant' or otherwise. The nearest possibilities are *Sixteen Famous American Plays* (a 'Giant') and *Six Modern American Plays* (a 'Regular').

numbers of *The Mask*, Gordon Craig's paper,[118] and novels, stuck among them. There were also one or two of the King Penguin books among them. I noticed John Ramsbottom's *Poisonous Fungi*. I took it out. Mary turned and saw me.

"That book belonged to Stella," she said, with a shadow passing over her face, "I'm afraid though that it didn't do her any good."

On the fly-leaf, in a round schoolgirl hand there was the name, "Stella Mortimer". I looked through the book. Judging from the first-rate descriptions and illustrations it seemed to me that it would have been a very foolish person who picked a Death Cap in mistake for a mushroom.

"By the way, Mary," I said, "Are you rehearsing this morning?"

"No," she replied, "I thought we might go for a walk. Would that suit you all right? I rather like the fields and woods at this time of the year."

"That would be lovely," I said, feeling a frightful beast for my deceitfulness, "perhaps we could collect a few mushrooms for me to take back to the old man. He says he can't stick these cultivated ones and asked me to bring him some. He said that if I picked any poison ones he'd soon enough weed them out."

Mary's face clouded. I could see that she was thinking of her last mushrooming expedition. I felt pretty terrible, and I felt more annoyed with the old man than ever. It was all very well, I said to myself, to ask someone else to do your dirty work for you. I only asked that I should not be asked to do that dirty work when it meant hurting the girl I loved. I should not have been surprised if Mary had refused to co-operate.

"All right, Max dear," she said, "I suppose there is no point in avoiding a place for ever because it has unhappy associations. We'll go mushrooming."

As we walked along between hedges heavy with sloes and the red leaves of the maples, I thought I might as well try and straighten out the rest of the thing that was nagging in my mind.

"When you and Stella went out that morning, Mary darling," I said, "I believe you had Arthur Loftus with you, hadn't you?"

She creased her brows. "Why, yes," she said in a surprised voice, "so we had. He helped us pick mushrooms for a few minutes and then he drifted off. He said he was not bucolic enough for that kind of amuse-

118 Edward Henry Gordon Craig (1872-1966) was a major influence on 20th century theatre and edited *The Mask*, the first international theatre magazine, from 1908-1929.

ment. Who told you?"

"Eric Owen," I said. There seemed to be no reason for me to cover him up.

"Oh, Eric," she said, with a half-laugh, "he loathes Arthur worse than anyone on earth. He would gladly fry him in oil if he had the chance. You see, when Stella was just starting, she met Arthur, who at that time, when there was a shortage of men, was doing quite well and she fell for his talk about what a big fellow he was and all the rest of it. She had an affair with him and it didn't last very long, for she quickly discovered that he was just a bag of wind, and that he was no real good as an actor or as a person. However, Arthur would never let her forget it, and Eric who's a sweet person, and who had a terrific thing about Stella, loathed his guts."

It seemed to me that everyone was tied up with everyone else. I saw that, if there was any truth in Douglas's story, the truth would only be found out through a tangled web.

"But look here," I said, "Eric had an idea that maybe Arthur picked a Death Cap and put it among the mushrooms with the idea that it would hurt Stella. Maybe he didn't know how poisonous it was, and just meant to make her feel rather sick. Eric says that he loathed Stella and would have liked to hurt her. What do you think?"

Mary frowned. At each alteration of her expression I felt that I loved her more and more. She kicked idly at a hanging head of knapweed by the roadside. A half-grown toad lolloped slowly across the road in front of us. I thought it was funny the way I noticed little things like that.

"Well," she said slowly, "it could be that way. But if Arthur had done a thing like that he might, for all he knew, have poisoned everyone in the house. Of course, if he was only going to make Stella sick, so far as he knew, he might have risked making everyone else sick as well." A sudden idea struck her. "You know, Max darling," her voice was serious, "Eric *may* be right. I've suddenly remembered that, after the party, although he was given mushrooms on toast Arthur ate none of them. He said he wasn't feeling hungry and went and got himself another drink."

Her voice was rather excited as she went on, "You see, if he had played a trick like that, he would not have risked eating anything which would make him sick himself. Then, when it turned out that Stella was seriously ill, he would have been afraid to own up that the cause was his own foolish trick. I wouldn't be at all surprised if that was the answer to the whole thing. But," her voice was sombre, "it doesn't matter now. It can't bring Stella back to life. It wouldn't do any good to try and pin things on Arthur, would it?"

I made no comment. If Stella had been the victim of a practical joke on the part of Arthur, I thought the best thing that could be done was to clear it up as quickly as possible. Once Douglas's story got into circulation, and, knowing Douglas, I was sure it would get into circulation, the best thing that could happen would be that things should be straightened up so that nobody was under suspicion.

Mary climbed over a stile. Climbing over a stile is a thing which few people can do with grace, but somehow she managed it. I got over it awkwardly after her, feeling that I was rather a let-down after her way of negotiating the obstacle.

"Here we are," she said, waving her hand round the field, which sloped down steeply towards a stream at the bottom. "This is where we usually come to pick mushrooms."

I looked around the field. It looked like most fields where there are horses grazing. The grass grew in thick tufts around the patches of dung, and elsewhere it was short and neatly cropped. Along one side of the field there ran a wood. Remembering my promise to the Professor I made towards that. I noted, without thinking about it, that the wood contained many beech trees.

As we went towards the wood we found the grass plentifully besprinkled with the common field mushroom, in all stages of development. We picked these into a string bag which Mary had brought with her for the purpose. I must confess that, even though I knew we were gathering specimens of *Psalliota campestris*, the common field mushroom, I did not feel any anxiety to make a meal of them.

As the mushrooms were growing among clumps of horse dung, they were inclined to be covered with brownish scales. But, even so, I did not see how they could be confused with *Amanita phalloides*.

We drew nearer and nearer to the wood and then I saw the protruding egg-shape of a young *Amanita phalloides*. It might very well have been taken for a large button mushroom. Once it was grown no one could have mistaken it, olive capped and with a ragged base, but young like that, it certainly was rather deceptive. Before we left the field I noticed, even more deceptive, the white or brownish tinged *Amanita verna*.[119] Still, I thought

119 *Amanita verna*, or the Destroying Angel, is also a highly poisonous mushroom and was first described by Jean Baillard (1742-1793).

to myself, one warned by the King Penguin should not have been deceived. The gills were white and not the familiar pink or, in the full-grown, brown.

CHAPTER TEN

ALL IN ONE BAG

I MORE or less threw the bag of fungi at the old man. He did not seem surprised by my greeting but caught it with an agility which was unsuspected by most of those who knew him.

"Here you are," I said crossly, "here are your *Amanita* this and your *Amanita* that. I hope you enjoy them. I hope they poison you."

I had arrived at Liverpool Street Station[120] in a bad temper. There may seem nothing unusual in this, as nobody has ever been known to arrive at that station in a good temper, but I was in a worse temper than anyone else on the train. If anyone had disagreed with me I would have fought them just to prove that I was worse than they were.

As a restful time my period in the country had been a damned flop. The only peaceful time I'd had was when I was mushrooming with Mary, and then the thought of Stella's death had been weighing down on us like a thunder cloud. The rest of the time various people had hung around Mary like bees around a plant. I had barely had a chance to get a word in edgeways. They had been so much better at the professional chatter than I was, and they knew all the *dramatis personæ* of their gossip in a way I could never hope to do. In fact I'd felt pretty well out of things.

All the same, I realised as soon as I'd spoken that it was not fair of me to vent my spleen upon the old man. He hadn't grumbled when he was told I was going away and I had no cause to curse him. So, with as good a grace as I could summon up, I apologised.

I told him about the innocent remarks of the faunish Mr. Owen. He thought them over carefully.

120 Liverpool Street Station was built in 1874 on the site of the first dedicated psychiatric institution, Bethlem Royal Hospital, from which the word *bedlam* is derived.

"Umm," he said slowly, "I think that that young man, Arthur Loftus, will need to answer a few questions. The Bishop, who's bin doin' a little research into the question is undoubtedly o' the opinion that there was indeed some funny business about the mushrooms, but he don't seem to think there's much he can do about it. He's comin' round here shortly an' I'm goin' to try an' knock a little public spirit into his fat head."

He offered me a pint of beer, by way of a sign that I was forgiven for my rudeness. He'd have offered it to me, anyway, even if he'd been hopping mad with me, so it didn't mean much. The way he offered it, though, showed his good intentions.

The Chief Inspector looked more weary than usual. His smooth plump face was unruffled by the cares of the world, but his eyelids drooped almost shut. I knew this as an indication that he expected that he would have a tough time with the old man. It was a sort of wall of defence which he put up as an excuse for taking no action on anything, which, privately, he might think needed some action.

"Hullo, John," he said in a listless voice, "what are you wanting this time? Have you found some new unsolved problem which you want to make me work on?"

The old man glowered at him. He blew out his cheeks and let out a gust of sound.

"Pah!" he boomed, "ye know as well as I do what I want t'see ye about. That girl was murdered or there was some kinda hankypanky. Ye know she ate mushrooms out o' a basket where there couldn't ha' bin any thunderin' *Amanita* o' any sort whatever. What I wanna know is what the blinkin' hell ye intend to do about it. What I wanna know is your official as well as yer private opinion o' the matter. Look at these objects Max has brought me. What d'ye think o' 'em?"

The Chief Inspector looked at the Professor sleepily over the thin edge of his brandy glass.

"It's all very well for you, John," he was apologetically quiet, "to think that I can take action on any case, merely because I'm morally certain that there is something wrong. As matters stand at the moment, even if we knew who had supplied that Death Cap thing we would still be unable to take any official action. Say, for instance, that young man Loftus was responsible for it – even if he meant it as a stupid and thoughtless joke he would be unlikely to admit his action. The tragic result will have frightened him into a state where he will be quite convinced that, if he was to confess, he would immediately be arrested and tried for murder. The way things are, John, there is absolutely nothing upon which the police can take action."

I thought the old man was about to explode. Instead he took a long pull at his quart tankard. He laid it down and glowered unhappily at the Chief Inspector.

"Uhhuh," he said slowly, "I see yer point. Ye can't take action till ye're sure that there's bin a crime committed, an' in this case, whatever ye may feel privately, there's no evidence for ye to start workin' wi'. That dam' coroner wi' his ideas about the holy profession o' medicine has pretty well gummed up the works as far as ye're concerned professionally."

"On the other hand," the Bishop was placatory, "I can, so as to speak, hold an unofficial watching brief and try to get more information for you to put together. After all, young Max here is in an ideal position to gather information about these people. He knows them and he knows the peculiar life they lead. Oh, by the way," his eyelids dropped further down on his cheeks, "you might be interested to know that that journalist fellow, Alec Dolittle, was also down at Linton during the last few days. He had been turning a penny or two by going round the different repertory theatres around London, writing them up for one of the dailies," he named a newspaper which made a point of 'culture' in the same way that others make a point of sport. "He could quite easily have gathered some of these toadstools when he was there and have brought them back to town with him."

"Hell's bells," the Professor was annoyed, "is there anyone in that party who has spent an honest time in London, just gettin' drunk an' not wanderin' round the countryside in places where he could ha' found *Amanita*?"

I looked at him enquiringly. So far as I knew only Arthur Loftus and now Alec Dolittle had been in a position to get hold of the poison fungi.

"Um," the old man grunted, "I bin doin' a bit o' research while ye bin tearin' around the place lookin' after yer lady. I found that young Newsome had bin down in Bucks[121] for a couple o' days, stayin' wi' his mother, an' that Harold Ironside had bin walkin' in the country tryin' to make up his mind to propose to Stella Mortimer. So far as I can see, the only one who couldn't ha' picked the damn things is Roger Sharon."

He sniffed expressively. I wondered what he was thinking about.

---

121 i.e. Buckinghamshire

"I don't suppose," I said guardedly, "that you are thinking that, because he has a sort of alibi, Roger Sharon was the one who killed Stella? If you are I may say that I don't believe you. I'd as soon believe that I'd done it myself or that Mary had done it as believe that. You saw how cut up he was, didn't you?"

"I'm not thinkin' anythin'," the Professor protested. "Why can't ye allow me to gather me facts wi'out thinkin' I'm drawin' wild conclusions from 'em before I've had time to let 'em settle an' digest? No, Max, if this is a murder, an' what yer friend Mr. Owen makes it look as though it might only be the result o' a practical joke, then we ha' not so far got the slightest lead. I'm just thinkin', tho', that we might go an' ask Mr. Loftus a few questions in the mornin'. He might, if he was the joker, gi' way under a little gentle pressure an' that might gi' us a lead if he's not. That sounds kinda muddled, but ye see what I mean?"

I nodded my head. The Chief Inspector took a sip of his brandy.

"By all means, John," he said amiably, "go ahead and see what you can discover. I may say that I do not think that you have the slightest chance of proving that anyone killed Miss Mortimer with malice aforethought, but there's no harm in your trying. You see what I mean, don't you? If this is a murder case, and it's a very big IF, it is as near perfect as you can make it. The only thing that has prevented it passing as a most unfortunate accident is the existence of that basket of cultivated mushrooms, and even there we have no evidence that one or two mushrooms out of the basket the girl picked may not have got mixed up with them. After all, we are going on the assumption that the story told us by that young man, who was admittedly drunk, is accurate."

The Professor, who had stumped over to the barrel in the corner to get some beer, turned his head and glared.

"That," he boomed, "is one o' the things I'm willin' to bet me trouser buttons on – just because he was drunk. If he'd bin sober I'd ha' said he was imaginin' the whole thing, but he was in that state o' drunkenness, just woken out o' a stupor, where everythin' around him would seem as clear as if it had bin thrown on a screen wi' a magic lantern. He would be quite positive that he hadn't left any o' the field mushrooms on the table, because he'd have a dead clear picture o' the table top lookin' absolutely empty."

It seemed to me that there was a great prospect of the Professor and the Chief Inspector chewing over the case all night. I felt rather tired, with the tiredness that only comes on those who have been forced to use

Liverpool Street Station.

I said good-night and wandered up the stairs to my room. In spite of the fact that I'd only been away for two nights, the poltergeist seemed to have been busy. Six volumes of *Curtis's Botanical Magazine* [122] were sitting on the end of my bed. The last time I'd seen them they had been in their places in the shelves in the hall. I picked them up and placed them precariously on the top of my bookshelf. I was too tired to take them down again. I washed and crawled into bed.

I did not get to sleep for a long time, as I kept on trying to make sense of the murder, *if* it was a murder, and I was not sure that it was. I wondered how much of my inclination to believe that Stella had been murdered was due to the fact that Professor Stubbs was always convinced that any death at all out of the ordinary was a murder which had been especially arranged for his benefit. Anyhow, I thought finally, we'll get a bit more information in the morning when we see Arthur Loftus. I fell asleep and dreamed of Mary, of Mary free from all the theatrical people who always seemed to get in the way when I wanted to talk to her.

The old man seemed to be in no hurry in the morning. He was wearing his loud tartan dressing-gown when I got down and was sitting at his desk answering letters from various colleagues. He is an appallingly bad correspondent, who leaves most of his letters for months, until they have answered themselves. It is part of my job, so I was pleased to see him so usefully occupied.

Breakfast passed pleasantly, without any of the usual bickering across the toast and coffee. After breakfast, the old man dressed and helped me with one or two points in my own work, which I had been neglecting, and which was consequently nagging at my conscience, or whatever I have that does duty for one.

When finally we left the house I noticed it was near opening time. The Professor drove his Bentley with his usual carefree abandon which makes me curl up inside myself. He really can frighten me in that damned car. When I protest he looks at me in surprise and points out that he certainly has occasionally hit something, but he's never hit a person yet nor has he

---

122 William Curtis (1746-1799) founded *The Botanical Magazine; or Flower Garden Displayed* in 1781 and it is now the longest running botanical magazine in the world. After his death the title was altered to *Curtis's Botanical Magazine* under the editorship of John Sims, with a second, short-lived change to *The Kew Magazine* between 1984 and 1994.

killed any of his passengers. I do not want to be the first on his list.

When we arrived at Mecklenburgh Square we found Roger Sharon busy painting. He was at work on a small oil which looked like a cross between a Torres García[123] and a Klee. It wasn't very good. I always feel sorry for Roger, as he really is so keen on painting and yet he just fails to be a good painter himself. His work is honest and good in its way, but somehow it fails to impress the spectator the way that he is impressed by one of the painters whom Roger admires so much.

He seemed to be pleased to see us. I must say that I wouldn't have been pleased in his position. After all the old man takes up a lot of space in pure bulk and he fills the rest of it with his voice.

I asked if we could see Arthur Loftus.

"I think he went out a few moments ago," Roger replied, "You might try his room though. It's upstairs. The one to the left of the top of the stairs. If he's not there you'll probably find him having a drink at *The Lamb*, unless someone's standing him drinks in the *Arts* or somewhere."

I went up the stairs leaving the old man talking to Roger. Arthur Loftus was not in his room. It looked as though it had been hit by a whirlwind, but I guessed that was just the way he liked living. The bed was not made and the sheets could, with some advantage, have been changed several months previously. There was a faintly sweet and sickly smell of fug in the room. I walked across it and opened the window.

On a low table in front of the window there were several books. Most of them had the plain blue covers of French's acting editions,[124] and the others were mostly plays, some of them printed and others in type-script. I noticed that most of the type-scripts were pretty thin cue-copies, their thinness giving some indication of the parts which Arthur Loftus took. In heaving open the window I knocked some of these papers on to the floor. As I bent to pick them up I saw the virulent green and red on yellow of the King Penguin book on poisonous fungi.

Of course, I told myself, there was no reason why Arthur Loftus should not have a copy of the book. After all he also had James Laver's one on

123 Joaquín Torres García (1874-1949) was a Uruguayan painter, writer and academic who created the Constructive Universalism style.

124 Samuel French (1821-1898) started his publishing activities in New York but after a visit to London in 1859 he formed a partnership with Thomas Hailes Lacey which was to become the most successful theatrical publisher in Great Britain.

costumes[125] and Max Beerbohm's *Poets' Corner.*[126] But he did not strike me as the sort of man who would have any interest in anything that grew, unless he saw it in a vase or in a florist's window. And, it occurred to me, it was quite likely that, hearing that Stella was suffering from poisoning from a fungus, he had seen the book and had gone and bought it to find out exactly what was the matter. I told myself that there was no reason why I should grow so suspicious just because a man had spent two shillings on a book which did not seem to fit in with his interests. I supposed it was just that I didn't like Arthur. I would never make a good detective, as I was too full of suspicions.

As I left Arthur Loftus's room the next door opened and Douglas Newsome popped out a mournful face which did not brighten at the sight of me.

"Hullo, Max," he said sadly, "Are you looking for Arthur? He went out some time ago. I don't expect he will come back unless he fails to persuade someone to buy him a meal."

I went on down the stairs as Douglas did not invite me in. As I went it dawned on me that if Arthur had killed Stella he really was carrying meanness to its peak. He hadn't even bought poison, but had picked it growing wild. That seemed to be too much to believe.

---

125 James Laver (1899-1975) wrote, and contributed to, a number of books on costume and fashion. This was probably *English Costume of the Nineteenth Century,* published by A. & C. Black in 1929, or *English Costume of the Eighteenth Century*, published by A. & C. Black in 1931.

126 Max Beerbohm (1872-1956) was a celebrated parodist and caricaturist. *Poet's Corner* was his second book of caricatures and was published by William Heinemann in 1904.

CHAPTER ELEVEN

NUTS IN MAY

WE LOCATED Arthur in *The Lamb*. He was sitting on a small tilting seat by himself, drinking half a pint of mild.

"'Ullo," the old man was breezy, "What're ye having? Beer?"

"If you don't mind," Arthur's voice was not friendly, "I would rather have a whisky."

The old man did not turn a hair. He ordered a large whisky and two pints of bitter. He managed to wedge his capacious form into one of the narrow seats. He beamed at Arthur with the friendliness of a grizzly bear watching its prospective lunch disporting and getting nearer to a place where it could not escape.

"I was wantin' to see ye," he said with disengaging frankness. The dead blue eyes of Arthur Loftus indicated that the desire was not what could have been called mutual.

"I was hearin' ye were down in the country an' that ye helped the girls gatherin' mushrooms? Eh?"

Arthur nodded his head. His face gave no indication of his thoughts.

"Yes," he said dispassionately, "I went out with them, but I only picked one or two mushrooms. I am not really suited for such bucolic pursuits. I wouldn't know a mushroom from the most poisonous fungus that there ever was."

I looked at him. He seemed very sure of himself. I thought I would put a spoke in his wheel.

"Yet," I spoke softly, "you have the Penguin book on poison fungi in your room?"

"So you've been poking among my things, have you? The great detective," his tone was not as offensive as his words, "Did you find anything else of interest? Oh, you needn't look surprised. I know that you and this man," he

115

gestured languidly at the Professor, "think that Stella was poisoned intentionally. If you found a book on poison fungi in my room it might interest you to know where I got it, mightn't it?"

"Where did you get it then?" I demanded.

"From Douglas. He collects all the King Penguins that he can find. He has the one on edible toadstools[127] too. But when I heard that Stella was suffering from fungus poisoning I thought I'd like to know what it could be and, seeing the book in a shop window, I thought I might as well borrow it from Douglas as I knew he had it and, after all, two bob is two bob."

How very typical, I thought; it was just like Arthur to want to know something and borrow rather than buy to find it out. He was looking at us in an unfriendly manner. The old man picked up his glass and slid it across the counter. He really was treating Mr. Loftus with the utmost courtesy.

"Mmhum," he pursed his lips, "so ye're not o' a bucolic nature, I can take it, Mr. Loftus?"

"You certainly can take it that way," Arthur was thawing slightly under the influence of two large whiskies, "I wouldn't know a bulrush from a cowslip if I was to meet them in the open. These sorts of things don't interest me. I'm interested in people and not in things."

He sipped at his whisky and seemed to be thinking. I could see that his face was taking on a spiteful twist.

"Why," he asked slowly, "don't you ask what Douglas knows about the things? It's the sort of thing he would know about. He likes playing the rather more scientific Wordsworth. He knows the Latin names of plants and he knows where to find them. His favourite poet is a chap called Andrew Young[128] who is also a botanist. Silly stuff I call it."

The old man blew out his frog-cheeks.

"Bah! sir," he exploded, "Ye don't know what ye're talkin' about. Young is a first rate man – has seen more wild plants in this country than anyone else an' writes dam' good poems. Keep to yer own subjects an' ye may talk sense."

---

127 *Edible Fungi*, also by John Ramsbottom, was published in 1943 and was the thirteenth in the King Pengunin series. The reference to edible toadstools is an odd one as it is generally used as a non-scientific term for poisonous mushrooms.

128 Andrew John Young (1885-1971) was a Scottish poet and clergyman who was originally ordained in the United Free Church of Scotland but later joined the Anglican ministry. He appeared in the anthology *Modern Scottish Poets*, published by Faber & Faber in 1946, along with Ruthven Todd.

"Oh all right," Arthur was sulky, "I was just trying to help you. You see you don't know anything at all. Stella was a little bitch. She was a bloody good actress but that didn't prevent her being a bitch. She had affairs all round town – how the hell do you think she managed to live? – and Douglas was one of these affairs. She had her eye on Roger; he'd got some money and would not be too exacting as a husband. To tell the truth there are a lot of people who are glad that she's dead. After all, if she'd married Roger do you think he'd have continued to run his house as a sort of doss-house? Not likely. Stella'd have seen that we all cleared out."

So far as I could see this was not getting us anywhere and the old man was just wasting money by turning it into whisky and pouring it into Arthur Loftus. Myself, I'd like to have brewed up some *Amanita phalloides* and given him a nip of that.

"Of course," he went on pensively, "it wouldn't have mattered to me if Stella had married Roger. I'm leaving anyhow. I've got a job and there seems to be some chance of there being a future in it. But if Roger and Stella had got tied up, several people would have been going around looking for a place to lay their heads. Douglas, for instance, would never have found anywhere so comfortable again, and Alec Dolittle would have had to do a bit more work. I don't know, of course, about Harold Ironside. Stella might have liked having him around as the royal eunuch. Roger would never have suspected anything."

It seemed to me that Mr. Loftus did not really like his friends. So far as I could see he had one great passion in his young life and that was the well-being of Arthur Loftus. I was getting restive. The old man seemed to be quite happy sitting there listening to the stream of gossip which was pouring from the *cloaca maxima* [129] which Arthur called his mouth. Most of the gossip I knew already and the rest of it was hardly worth the trouble of retelling.

I sank my beer and bought another round. Since the old man was buying Arthur whisky I did the same. I supposed there was a reason for it. There usually is a reason for most of the odd things the old man gets up to. Sometimes I think he's playing Sherlock Holmes with the good old-fashioned method in his madness, but when I've suggested that to him he's been so vociferously indignant that I have ceased showing my suspicions openly.

---

129 The *cloaca maxima* was the sewer system of ancient Rome.

Arthur Loftus sat there with his magnolia-bud face screwed into an expression of passive suffering. His face said plainly that he did not suffer fools with any gladness and was only putting up with us for the sake of the drink.

"Uhhuh," the old man rumbled over the lip of his beer mug, "an', if ye don't mind me askin', what's yer own opinion o' the case?"

Arthur seemed to weigh the question carefully in the balance of his mind, placing a pennyweight here or there to make the scales level.

"Oh," his voice was mildly pleased, as if flattered that anyone had thought it worth asking his opinion, "I'm glad that you have asked me that. Of course, I don't pretend to be a detective," he could not quite manage to keep the sneer out of his tone, "but, as an intelligent person, I cannot help forming my own conclusions."

He paused again and seemed to be selecting his words like a compositor selecting type.

"I'm not sure," he went on, and there was something sly about him, "that I should start voicing my suspicions at this stage. But, if you ask me," this seemed to me silly as the old man had just asked him, "I'd look into Alec Dolittle a little bit more closely. He's the sort of fellow who knows which side his bread is buttered all right and he's ruthless enough when anything gets in his way."

He rose to his feet, tipping the last trickle of whisky down his throat.

"Thank you for the drink. I'm afraid I must be going now. I've got work to do, you know?"

We didn't know, but we made no effort to hold on to him. I was personally pretty sick of his company and I think the old man was just beginning to get bored.

"Um," the old man grumbled, "what d'ye make o' him? I'd like a nice pint o' bitter to wash the taste away meself." The idea seemed a good one so we had some more beer. The longer I live with the Professor the greater my cubic capacity becomes.

"It seemed to me," I said ponderously, "that Mr. Loftus doesn't like his friends and that he's hiding something. What do you think?"

"Umph, glumph," the old man gurgled through his beer, "I'm inclined to agree wi' ye there. I don't think that there's anythin' in his idea that we'd better look into Dolittle. It's just some sort of spite which he was getting off his chest, and I'd say that he's astute enough to ha' his suspicions o' someone else an' was tryin' to throw us Dolittle as a kind o' Christian for our lions, in the hope that they won't eat whoever it is he's kinda marked down as his own prey. Eh? What d'ye think o' that?"

I thought there was little doubt that Arthur was, in fact, hiding something, so I started wondering who he could he protecting, if that was the right word for it.

The old man had drawn a crumpled envelope and the short stub of a pencil from his pocket and was busily engaged in making notes. In spite of the shortness of his bit of pencil and the fact that he was leaning the envelope on his knee his writing was as small and neat as usual. He leaned back in his cramped chair and passed the envelope to me.

"More beer?" he enquired, and ordered it without waiting for my answer, "Ye see what I done here? I just jotted down the names o' those who might conceivably ha' killed Stella wi'out any thought o' motive. Now ye try an' put in yer motives."

The list of possibilities was not impressive and I did not see that there was much to be done with it. I said so and he leaned over towards me, nearly upsetting the marble-topped table upon which our beers stood.

"Well, now," he said slowly, "suppose we begin wi' the first name, an' there's no need for ye to look so dam' indignant. Ye may ha' fallen for the lady, but ye must remember that the coppers won't ha', an' we got to approach the affair in the same way. Mary Winstone. Now she certainly had the opportunity o' pickin' the *Amanita* an' puttin' it in the basket wi' the field mushrooms an' in that drunken party she could no doubt ha' slipped it into Stella's meal, but we don't see that she's got any reason to do that an', for the moment, we can clear her. Eh?"

"Thank you," I said in a voice that was decidedly ungrateful. I thought it was pretty tough when I found that I was mixed up in murder so often without having Professor Stubbs suspecting the girl I was going to marry, or at least whom I hoped to marry, though things hadn't got as far as that yet. I thought of Mary and glowed within myself.

"Now," the old man was continuing, "we take young Newsome. Well, he'd as much opportunity o' gatherin' the mushrooms as the rest o' 'em. He was down in the country. He had more opportunity than the others for puttin' the *Amanita* into the girl's portion o' mushrooms on toast, an' he admits that he was kinda in love wi' her. So, ye see, he might very well ha' decided that if he didn't have her no one else would, an' ha' started out to make her suffer for slightin' him. But," his mumble was annoyed, "I must say that I don't see the boy in the part. He's anti-Byronic an' wouldn't be given to such extreme action. What d'ye think o' him?"

I did not think that Douglas had done the job of killing Stella and I said so. My own choice was Arthur Loftus. The old man disagreed with me and said that, while Arthur was holding something back, he did not think it was a confession of his guilt. I pointed out that once before I had been right in choosing someone I did not like as the murderer, even when Professor Stubbs had said that he could not be. He glared at me through the gap between his spectacles and his forehead.

"O' course," he said loudly and rudely, "If ye're goin' to start yer intuition business I can't do anythin' about it. Ye must remember that I go by facts an' not by feelin'. I got the scientific mind, I have." He was loudly indignant, "I'm a believer in experimental proof. Ye don't find me goin' around believin' in thin's which I can't prove. I wait till I got all the facts an' then I start deducin' from 'em."

He snorted as he drunk his beer and promptly choked, noisily and with a considerable explosion. I beat him heartily between the shoulder blades. The disturbance in the pub was almost as great as if the door had opened and an iguanodon had walked in. When he had sufficiently recovered he snorted again, taking care that this time his gullet was cleared for action. He looked at me as if I had been responsible for his choking. I was not impressed.

"Now," he rumbled, "ye can take a look at Harold Ironside. Maybe he'd ha' bin so dam' sick at losin' the girl that he'd ha' made up his slow mind that if he wasn't to have her no one else was to. Eh? Um. No. I can't say that I see his mind workin' that way, meself. Rather I'd say that he might be inclined to consider that Roger Sharon was in the way an' ha' tried to get him out o' it. Even then I think he'd ha' chosen some other weapon than poison." His eye brightened as he said this and I knew that I was in for a short lecture. I composed myself to let it drip in through my ears. "Now, there's more tommy rot talked about poison than about anythin' else. They say that poison's a woman's weapon. If it was, the lookout for yer girl 'ud be pretty bleak, eh? But me, I say that poison could be used by anyone at all. It don't make a noise an' it ain't messy aroun' the house. What ye don't use is easily disposed o' afterwards. So when I say that I don't think that Harold Ironside 'ud ha' used poison I'm not sayin' that he was incapable o' usin' the stuff – it's just that I don't think he has the wits. Now I don't know as much about these people as ye do, but it don't seem to me that Ironside 'ud be much o' a tactician, eh? He's the sort o' feller who goes at a thing hell bent on gettin' there an' stumbles over or kicks out o' his way an obstacle he comes across, eh?"

Relieved that the lecture had been such a short one, I nodded my head. It certainly did not seem likely that Harold would have killed Stella, though he might, at that time, have killed Roger. My inside felt like the blue lagoon – all water and precious little land. I felt that I could do with a nice lunch and was just about to suggest it. Unfortunately, the old man got his order for more beer in before I could speak. I resigned myself to waiting a few minutes more.

"Then," he said deeply, "ye come to Roger Sharon." He paused for a moment, and I wondered what absurdity he was huddling up in his mind. "Well, he's the kinda complex character who might very well ha' done this murder. Ye see, he may ha' bin led by his emotions into proposin' a marriage which he could not ha' wanted to take place. Maybe Stella Mortimer got him in a position where he felt that his freedom was threatened. From what her friends say o' her, she seems to ha' bin a young woman o' some determination, an' if she'd made up her mind that she wanted Sharon, well, I doubt if he'd ha' stood a chance against her. An' feelin' pretty desperate he might well ha' determined to get her out o' the way. Once he'd done the deed he'd ha' had no bother in disconnectin' himself from the murderer, an' he'd ha' shown a perfectly genuine grief an' unhappiness. What d'ye think o' that?"

"Well, I think it is nonsense. After all Roger is living to-day and not in a mid-Victorian atmosphere, and to-day you don't need to go to the extent of murdering anyone to get them out of your emotional way. After all the road to the Divorce Courts is broad enough and is trodden by enough people so that there's little chance of your losing your way. Even if Roger had felt himself in a position where he wanted to escape from marrying Stella, and had, at the same time, felt that he had to go through with it, he would only have needed to make a temporary affair of the thing. If everything that people say about her was right, Stella's morals were not such that a man, really eager for a divorce, would have needed to look far for evidence. But, apart from all that, I consider that your case makes nonsense. I just don't believe that Roger murdered Stella and if you were to produce a water-tight case I still wouldn't believe it. I just can't see him in the part and I think you are just erecting Aunt Sallies for your own amusement. To put it bluntly I don't believe you know anything!"

Professor Stubbs chewed at his lower lip. He looked at me over his beer and sighed.

"Um," he said slowly, "Maybe ye're right, Max boy. Maybe I'm an old fool. Let's go get some food, for I can see yer belly workin' in yer face."

CHAPTER TWELVE

THE DEVIL WHO IS DEATH[130]

WHEN I got back to Hampstead in the middle of the afternoon I found there was a message for me. It was written in Mrs. Farley's painstaking round hand and was propped up on top of the telephone so that I could not miss it. I picked it up and unfolded it.

"Miss Winstone rang," it said, "and says that unexpectedly she has an evening in town. Will you meet her at Mr. Sharon's house?"

Would I meet her at Roger's? By God, I told myself, I'd go all the way to the moon to meet her.

The afternoon went fast. I did a little work on a paper which I was writing. The old man sat at his desk and seemed to be reading his way right through Darlington and Janaki's *Chromosome Atlas*.[131] This is almost a dictionary and yet the old man seemed to be as engrossed in it as he would have been in the latest detective story by Michael Innes.[132]

When I got to Roger's I was disappointed and, if the truth be told, slightly annoyed to find that I was not after all, to have an evening with Mary by myself. There was a note stuck to the door telling me that they were all drinking in the back bar of *The Café Royal*.[133] Rather sadly I walked

---

130 This appears in Christopher Smart's (1722-1771) *Jubilate Agno*: "For he counteracts the Devil, who is death, by brisking about the life."

131 The *Chromsome Atlas of Cultivated Plants*, by Cyril Dean Darlington and Edavaleth Kakkat Janaki Ammal, was first published in 1945 by George Allen & Unwin.

132 The most recent Michael Innes story would have been *The Weight of the Evidence* published by Victor Gollancz in 1944.

133 *The Café Royal* was established in 1865 by Daniel Nicholas Thévenon, a bankrupt wine merchant who fled from France to London and adopted the name Daniel Nichols. It was famous for the extent and quality of its wine cellar and was a favoured haunt of the rich and famous.

down to Guilford Street[134] and caught a taxi. It was pretty damnable that I was not able to see a girl by herself when I wanted to do so. I expected that they would all be there. It was too much to hope that there would only be one or two of them standing or sitting round the bar.

I was right. They were all there. Mary was sitting between Roger and Arthur. Harold was standing rather gloomily at the bar, slowly sinking a pint of Pimm's[135] while listening to Alec Dolittle. Douglas Newsome was doodling on a scrap of paper.

"Hullo, Mary," I said as cheerfully as I could manage, "It is nice to see you so unexpectedly. How did you manage it?"

"Oh, Max, darling, the two sisters have collected doses of 'flu and as one of them is in the play and the other stage manages the show, it just had to be put off. Oh, darling, I am so glad to see you."

The words were all right, but the tone was just the tone of theatrical politeness. The word darling meant no more than "oy, you" in ordinary language. I looked to see what the others were drinking and made my way up to the bar. It was a damned expensive round. Mary and Harold were on Pimm's, Douglas was drinking gin – plain gin with no frills – and Arthur and Roger were on whisky. The hell on it, I said to myself, and made mine a large brandy. I realised that I'd forgotten Alec, but he was easily dealt with as he was drinking lager.

Alec was telling a story, and I hadn't the slightest idea what it was all about.

"And so," he said with an expressive grimace, "the pudding came out all covered with newsprint in reverse. A veritable printer's pie."[136]

Harold did not laugh. "I suppose it was something to do with the ink," he said solemnly.

"I suppose so," Alec equalled him in solemnity, "but then you never know, do you?"

134 Guilford Street runs east from Russell Square to Gray's Inn Road and passes by Mecklenburgh Square.

135 Pimm's is a spirit-based fruit cup, particularly popular in the South of England and at events such as Wimbledon, Henley and Glyndebourne, which was first produced by James Pimm (1798-1866) in 1823. At the time of the story there were three cups available: No.1, based on gin; No.2, based on brandy; and No.3, based on whisky.

136 A printer's pie is a jumble of lead type that has been knocked over, dropped or otherwise disturbed.

"No," Harold replied. It did not seem to me that there was much future in this conversation and I was not archæologist enough to dig after its past. I drifted across to Roger and Arthur, hoping to get a word in with Mary. It was a poor turn out for me. Arthur was gossiping madly about people of whom I knew nothing. It wouldn't have made any difference if I had known them, as the nicknames and Christian names would have mixed me up pretty quickly.

Roger looked very bored, but I might as well have talked against a factory whistle as have tried to slide a word past Arthur's gossip.

I drank my brandy rather too quickly and looked around. Nobody else was ready, so I thought I might as well do a bit of catching up. I had another large brandy. By the time I'd had the fourth brandy I began to feel that things were not really as bad as they seemed. Every now and again Mary smiled at me across the table, through the miasma of gossip, and I told myself there was something secret between us hidden in these smiles. I smiled back.

Alec was telling another story. Somehow I always seemed to come in late on his stories. This one, I gathered, was about a landlady he had had somewhere in Pimlico.[137]

"Well," he was saying, "my trouble was that I always got home after she did and it was all she could do to get through the front door, when she used to pass out like a log. So when I got home I used to have to scrum-down on the door and shove. I'd feel her sliding gradually up as I pushed and then there would come the moment of suspense. Would she topple sideways and block the entrance or would she go right over the top? I may say I got pretty expert in turning her over and I only got locked out once. After I'd got her like that I would edge my way through the door and then I'd catch hold of her – she weighed twenty stone if she was an ounce – and drag her a bit towards the door of her room. It depended how tired I was how far I got her. I only got her all the way once or twice. God, there were landladies in those days."

Neither of them laughed. Harold nodded a grave agreement with Alec's statement about the golden age of landladies. I began to feel that there must be something wrong with me. I thought of the smallish Alec

137 Pimlico contains many impressive Regency buildings and communal garden squares, and was laid out to a grid system by Thomas Cubitt (1788-1855) in the 1820s in an area to the south of Belgravia. Todd stayed in several boarding houses in Pimlico when he first moved to London.

hauling away on a woman-mountain and the idea amused me, but they were both as placid as owls during the daytime.

Arthur paused in his recital of scandal. Roger, relieved, said that he thought it was time we went into the dining-room and had a bite to eat.

Someone else thought we should have a last drink before dinner, so we proceeded to have a great many more drinks. In one way the drink was mellowing me, but in others I was gradually getting irritated. Firstly, I was annoyed that I was not having Mary to myself and, secondly, I thought that Arthur Loftus was being a damn sight too familiar with her. I noticed him whispering to her once or twice and when he did so she looked puzzled. It was all right, I knew, he was only telling her some extra choice piece of scandal which even he did not dare to spread aloud. But all the same I was annoyed.

All through dinner my dislike of Arthur grew greater. He seemed to take a positive pleasure in preventing my talking to Mary. I was landed between Harold and Roger and made small-talk with them. Like myself I did not think they were feeling over cheerful. I had not really known Stella Mortimer, but if I had I guessed I'd have been feeling and looking much as they did.

I suppose we all had rather too much drink. From the appearance of Douglas it was obvious that he had had too much. He let his eyes roll vacantly round the table and shuddered to himself. I was afraid that he might be sick. I thought I had better do something to take his mind off the convolutions of his stomach full of drink.

"You're very quiet, Douglas," I said, "what are you thinking? Is something worrying you?"

He pulled himself up behind the table, clutching at the white cloth and looked round the assembled company absently. When he spoke his voice was a low monotone.

"And now me-thinkes I could e'en chide my selfe
For doating on her beauty, tho' her death
Shall be revenged after no common action.
Does the Silke-worme expend her yellow labours
For thee? for thee does she undoe herself?"[138]

It could hardly have been called a happy quotation. Harold swore qui-

---

[138] From *The Revenger's Tragedy* (Act 3 Scene 5) by Cyril Tourneur (1575-1626), though also attributed to Thomas Middleton (1580-1627).

etly to himself and Roger glared. I heard Mary catch her breath, sharp and bitter, and I could have slaughtered Douglas for his tactlessness. I could have killed myself for bringing it out into the open.

"That's the stuff, Douglas," Alec exclaimed cheerfully. He was obviously drunk; I tried to kick him under the table but got Harold instead. "Do you know any more of it?"

"Plenty," said Douglas, briefly, interrupting a hiccough, "How will this do? I think it fits the scene to-night:

Drink and sing, and eat and laugh,
And so go forth to battle;
For the top of a skull and the end of a staff
Do make a ghostly rattle!"[139]

We managed to calm him down by getting him another drink. It seemed that even if he did get sick-drunk he'd be better that way than exploring the vasty hall of death[140] in his mind.

After we had finished eating we decided that we might as well carry the party to a pub, and so we drifted out into Glasshouse Street[141] and along Beak Street[142] to Old Compton Street[143] where we poured into *The Swiss*.[144] The place was crowded and even though, by terrific manœuvering I did manage to get next to Mary, I might have saved my energies. I could hardly hear myself think let alone hear what Mary said to me. There was no help for it. I would just have to make up my mind that it was a wasted evening out, and hope for better luck next time. Having made my decision, I did not bother about the rest of the party, but concentrated on enjoying myself as much as I could. I was contented when the sway of the crowd brought Mary close to me.

When *The Swiss* closed we drifted down an alley-way and found a little café still open. We went in and ordered coffee. We got seats all right, but even here it was noisy as a small Italian was playing *Ave Maria* on a piano

139 From *Maid Marian* by Thomas Love Peacock (1785-1866).
140 A phrase used by Matthew Arnold (1822-1888) in *Requiescat*.
141 Glasshouse Street may be named after the work of Windsor Sandys, who was active in the area and who, with his partner John Dwight, supplied stoneware to the Glass Sellers' Company from 1676.
142 Beak Street runs east from Regent Street towards Soho.
143 Old Compton Street lies in Soho and was named after Henry Compton, an English Bishop and Protestant dissenter.
144 *The Swiss Hotel* was designed by Williams and Hopton and built in 1890.

accordion with a great deal of verve and emotion. He was bald on top but, before starting to play, he tied his long side hair in a knot over the top of his head. As he played the hair gradually untied itself and slopped down the sides of his face. This was apparently the *pièce de résistance* of the café. In a corner near the door there sat a tough middle-aged man who looked like a burglar and probably was one. As the little Italian got really going on *Ave Maria* I noticed that large tears were rolling down the cheeks of this really tough character. It was an odd sight.

We sat in the café for quite a time, saying little and engrossed in our own thoughts. I wondered whether I was in Mary's thoughts, for, every time I looked over at her, she caught my eye and smiled. This would have pleased me more if I hadn't seen her doing the same to both Arthur Loftus and Roger Sharon.

When we left the café we wound our way to Leicester Square tube station and got our tickets. The others were going to Russell Square[145] while I was going to Belsize Park,[146] but I thought I might as well see them off and then wend my way through the underground passages to my own platform.

The platform was as crowded as *The Swiss* pub had been. It might even have been a bit more crowded. We swayed backwards and forwards, and we were not helped in our balance by the amount we had taken to drink.

What happened next will always be rather muddled in my mind. I felt the draught of strong air as the train drew near the station and at the same moment felt a tug at my coat from Douglas. He was staring up at the clock.

"What's a'clock?" he asked, rhetorically, and answered his own question, "It wants a quarter to midnight, and tomorrow's doomsday."[147]

The train swept into the station as we were looking up at the clock like a lot of fools, while at the same time we tried to keep our feet in the surge of humanity.

There was a horrible scream as the train drew level with us, and, without looking for him I realised that Arthur Loftus had gone straight down

145 Russell Square was built by James Burton in the early 1800s for the Duke of Bedford. It is a large garden square which lies to the east of the British Museum. Russell Square tube station is on adjoining Bernard Street and is a Grade II listed building.

146 Belsize is named after Belassis, the manor of Roger de Brabazon, Chief Justice to Edward III.

147 From *The Ivory Gate* by Thomas Lovell Beddoe (1803-1849).

under the very front of the train.

The driver did not have a chance. There was nothing he could have done. When they did get what remained of Arthur out from underneath the train it was not pretty. The only thing that prevented me from being damnably sick myself was that I had to look after Mary. I must say she took it pretty well. She was shaken and looked ill, but she was not the least hysterical. I wouldn't have blamed her if she had been. A fit of hysteria is a very fine defence against the more unpleasant things in life – or death.

There were questions in galore. It seemed to me that we would never have finished with questions. We answered this and we answered that. Finally we all gave our names and addresses and were permitted to depart. It was quite obvious from the demeanour of the officials that they were convinced that we had all been rolling drunk and had been ragging about on the edge of the platform.

They seemed to think that it was an accident caused partly by our drinking and partly by the congested state of the platform. I was not so sure myself. I dislike deaths that divide like amœba and produce twins. Also, I was beginning to get the feeling of the glass bottles hanging on the wall – if one green bottle should accidentally fall there'd be umpteen green bottles hanging on the wall.

There was a light under the professor's door when finally, with the help of a taxi, I managed to get home. I tapped on the door and received a noisy invitation to enter.

He was sitting up in bed, swathed in his tartan dressing-gown and a fur rug. On his head he was wearing a fur-lined flying helmet. I have rarely seen such a comic sight. The top of the bed was littered with odd volumes of *Curtis's Botanical Magazine*. So far as I could make out the old man was not concerned with these but was reading a thriller.

"Well," he looked at me over the shiny tops of his glasses, "What's bitin' ye? Ye look as though ye'd seen a ghost o' some kind, or as if someone had bin kickin' ye in the belly. What's up? Come on now spit it out. It won't improve by keepin' it."

As ordered, I spat it out. I did my best to give the old man an account of the evening. I frankly admitted that, being slightly on the peevish side, I had drunk a bit too much. I finished my story and waited for any comments he had to make.

"Umhum," he grunted from the corner of his mouth as he applied his vast and ferocious lighter to his filthy pipe, "I'm inclined to agree wi' ye, Max, for once. Ye don't just find violent accidental deaths growin' on every gooseberry bush in the garden. Things don't, in me own experience, happen in that way. I wonder," his voice was slow, "what made young Newsome start exclaimin' in that way at just that time."

"Oh," I said, "he was drunk and he'd been spouting quotations all the evening. I suppose he just looked at the clock and saw the time and the snatch from Beddoes's *Death's Jest Book*[148] came into his mind. He'd already let loose one piece of Beddoes earlier in the evening, as well as rather a choice piece from the *Revenger's Tragedy*."

All the same, having done my best to absolve Douglas I started to wonder to myself whether, after all, he had not been being clever. Say, I said to myself, he had discovered that Arthur Loftus had murdered Stella, he might very well have been warning him that he knew too much by that quotation from Tourneur. Any one of us could have pushed Arthur at that moment – we were all looking at the clock, not at Douglas. He might have done the trick as his revenge "after no common action." I told Professor Stubbs what I thought and he nodded his head wisely, like a fabulous owl.

"Maybe aye," he said, "an' then, on the other hand, maybe no. I wouldn't like to bet on it. After all, ye yerself ha' pointed out that the boy was what ye might call 'much obsessed wi' death' an' busy seein' 'the skull beneath the skin.'[149] Once ye start on that thin' ye find that yer mind starts pilin' up quotations at an appallin' rate – 'Cut is the branch that might have grown full straight,'[150] or, if ye'd rather 'Dear, beauteous Death! the jewel o' the just',[151] or anythin' else ye like. Once ye start, as I say, ye can hardly stop. It's the poems about death that stick in yer mind, not the ones about bein' happy an' gay."

For once in my life I found the perfect answer. It isn't often that I manage to get one up an the old man, but suddenly there came to me a snatch from *The Duchess of Malfi*, and I let him have it.

"O that it were possible we might
But hold some two dayes conference with the dead!
From them I should learne somewhat, I am sure

---

148 This was the nickname given to Beddoe's *Ivory Gate*.

149 From *Whispers of Immortality* by T.S. Eliot (1888-1965).

150 From *Doctor Faustus* (Act 5, Scene 4) by Christopher Marlowe (1564-1593).

151 From *They Are All Gone into the World of Light!* by Henry Vaughan (1621-1695).

I never shall know here."[152]

The old man admitted that I was one up on him. He chuckled hugely.

"Thank God, Max," he exploded, "that we can't. We'd ha' no blinkin' murders to solve an' what could the writers o' thrillers do for a livin'? Cripes, Max, I'd be bored."

"You'd be bored," I replied and then realised that we'd started to play T.S. Eliot's *Sweeney Agonistes.*[153] It seemed to me that the conversation was becoming a little bit on the recondite side. If this game of matching quotations went on much longer I felt that we'd never be able to speak in our own voices again. I began to feel a little like the lady at dinner in *Comus,*[154] surrounded by animal heads and voices. I changed the subject in the hope that that wouldn't be such a maddening thing.

"You see," I said hopefully, "perhaps Arthur was indeed the murderer of Stella and remorse coupled with drink had made him giddy so that he fell under the train. Or else, he may have thought that Douglas knew something about him and committed suicide. So far as I can make out the platform was so crammed with people that nobody is sure what happened. One old lady said she thought he swayed as if about to faint, but my private belief was that the said old lady had been boozing not wisely but too well and suddenly found herself in the middle of a death and couldn't keep her nose out of it. She looked the sort of old lady who likes funerals."

"Uhhuh," the old man picked up the discarded volume and buried his nose in it, "It'll keep, Max, and maybe yer mind'll be a bit clearer in the mornin' an' ye'll remember somethin' which may gi' us a bit o' a lead. As things are all this death does is to provide us wi' the same characters, less Arthur Loftus. Good-night."

There was obviously nothing more for me to say. I might have talked till my face was the colour of a mandrill's backside, but I'd have got no satisfaction from Professor Stubbs.

I said good-night and made my way up to my bedroom. That damned

---

152 From *The Duchess of Malfi* (Act 4, Scene 2) by John Webster (1580-1634).

153 This was Eliot's first, and unsuccessful, attempt at verse drama which was eventually published as *Sweeney Agonistes: Fragments of an Aristophanic Melodrama* by Faber & Faber in 1932. When Todd was in Mull in 1933 he wrote a rather juvenile attempt at a verse drama called *A Melodrama*, in which he quotes from *Sweeney Agonistes.*

154 *Comus: A Mask Presented at Ludlow Castle,* was written in 1634 by John Milton (1608-1674).

poltergeist seemed to have been loose again. I had to clear a large and mis-cellaneous collection of seventeenth century octavos from my bed before I could get into it.

So far as I could see the morning would bring no clarity to affairs. If it didn't I was not to blame. I shrugged a pair of mental shoulders and thought nicely of Mary till I fell asleep.

CHAPTER THIRTEEN

DESPAIRE, LAW, CHANCE, HATH SLAINE[155]

I was right. The morning brought nothing but Chief Inspector R. F. Bishop, as bland as a pope and as smooth and sleepy as a well-fed Persian cat.

"Hullo, Max," he greeted me wearily, "You been getting into trouble once more?"

"No, damn you," I was indignant, "if I can't go out for an evening's drinking with some friends without accidents happening it's not my fault. I'm damned if I see any reason why I should shut myself off from humanity because accidents like this happen. Would you like me to become a celibate monk?"

"Yes," said the Bishop simply. I saw that he wasn't in a mood where I could get under his skin. No matter what I said he'd be able to flatten me with the last word.

"Anyhow," I changed the subject, "what do you want to see me about? I'm a busy man who's supposed to be writing a learned paper on the subject of wheat."

"It's just you, Max," the Chief Inspector looked unhappy, "I don't know how it is, but it seems to me that too much happens when you are around. First there's the death of that girl Stella Mortimer – well you know as well as I do that that *might* have been an accident. It would have passed as one but for you and John Stubbs. Now, one of the people mixed up in that accident is mysteriously involved in another in Leicester Square underground station. I must say I don't like it. I've looked at the reports and they say that the platform was exceedingly crowded at the time and that, so far as they can see, there is no reason to label the occurrence as anything else than an

---

155 From *Holy Sonnets* by John Donne (1572-1631).

accident. But as I've said, I don't like it, Max, don't like it at all."

The Professor entered the room. He glowered at the Chief Inspector like a friendly bear inspecting its lunch.

"So ye don't like it, Reggie?" he rumbled, "Well, I can tell ye that I don't like it either. So far as I'm concerned the whole set-up stinks to high heaven – an' back again. Frankly I don't believe that people ha' convenient accidents when there's murder aroun', d'ye?"

The question was rhetorical, but the Bishop shook his head slowly. He looked very sad and weary.

"Uhhuh," the old man went on, "so ye see we got to act on the assumption that Arthur Loftus was either helped to his long home, or that he went there o' his own accord. The second supposition 'ull only hold water if he was the blinkin' murderer an' thought that someone had somethin' on him. If anyone had known anythin' which pointed to Loftus bein' the murderer they'd ha' pulled that rabbit out o' the bag by this time. As a group they none o' them strike me as the sort of people who'd be over reticent about a thin' o' that sort. Meself, I don't believe that Arthur was the thunderin' murderer. I think that he knew somethin', tho', an' he was holdin' it up his sleeve in the hope that it 'ud thumpin' well turn out to be o' benefit to Mr. Arthur Loftus. Ye know his character, eh? He was the collector o' gossip an' scandal – he was the feller who prided himself on bein' just a little bit *more* in the know than the next feller. A nice juicy bit o' scandal was like a new plant is to me – I mayn't be able to do anythin' wi' it at the moment, but I like havin' it around. Now ye can take a look at the collection on that dam' tube platform. It was the same blinkin' mixture as before. I think ye can exclude Max, here, from all suspicion o' having helped Loftus under the wheels o' the train. Eh, what d'ye say?"

The Chief Inspector looked at me through half-opened eyes. He shook his head solemnly.

"Well, John," he replied, "I suppose we'd better absolve him. But, as I was saying when you came in, I don't like the way that there always seems to be trouble whenever he goes on the loose. If I had my way I'd shut him up where he couldn't cause trouble – though, I suppose, even if you put him in a straight-jacket in an asylum, you'd find that the attendants would start killing one another off."

There didn't seem to be much that I could say by way of answer. It just seemed to be my luck that I was always around when there was trouble, bad trouble. If I'd thought it would have done any good I believe I'd have gone and had myself psycho-analysed to see if I could get it out of my system. I knew that there would be trouble wherever I went. It just seemed hellish tough that I, who wanted a quiet life, should be unable to get it.

"Now, Reggie," the old man was getting into his stride. He was walking up and down the room with the aimlessness of a polar bear parading the Mappin Terrace.[156] "I got no ideas," he glared at the Chief Inspector as if waiting to be contradicted, and seemed disappointed that there was no disagreement from that quarter. "I don't know who murdered Stella Mortimer, an' I ain't got the foggiest who done in Arthur Loftus. I can make out the sort o' a case against any one o' the people concerned but I still can't make a case which 'ull hold water against any one o' them in particular."

In spite of the earliness of the hour, when one of the Professor's strolls brought him near to the beer-barrel, he poured himself a quart. The Chief Inspector and I refused to partake of the stuff at that time.

Professor Stubbs dumped himself heavily in his large arm-chair. He took out his horrible little black pipe and went through the ritual of scraping the carbon deposit out of the bowl, cutting up some toxic-looking black plug and tamping it into place. Once he was comfortably surrounded by the noxious fumes he seemed happier.

"Trouble wi' this case," he exploded suddenly, "is that it's got no roots. We don't know enough about the backgrounds o' all these people. We don't know the reasons that might ha' led up to someone wantin' to murder Stella Mortimer. We can take it, I think, that Arthur Loftus knew somethin' and that what he knew was dangerous to the murderer. For I can't meself see him playin' the part o' first murderer. He hadn't got the guts or the imagination to think o' using *Amanita* either *phalloides* or *verna* – tho' why the blinkin' hell they should call it *verna* I don't know as it very rarely appears before the autumn. Even if Loftus had murdered the girl, he'd not ha' committed suicide – he was a young man wi' a fair conceit o' himself an' he'd ha' bin quite sure that he could ha' put it over on us. He thought that he was clever an' by God so he was – too thumpin' clever. All the same, it's a pity that he had to go, for he was a well from which we might ha' drawn plenty o' water – he'd ha' gi'n us all the facts we wanted about these people an' ha' bin pleased to do it – he'd a nice kinda spite which made him like hittin' out at those he called his friends. He would ha' told us what jealousies there were which might ha' flared up and who was the person he suspected. He was keepin' it under his hat, but he couldn't ha' kept it there for long. He'd a hole in the top o' his head and he just couldn't avoid talkin' through it."

This remark of the Professor's seemed to me to be in bad taste. I had a brilliant mental picture of the dead Arthur's head where it had been hit by some part of the mechanism of the train. I retched violently. The old man looked up at me in a surprised way.

"What's the matter wi' ye?" he demanded, blowing out his cheeks. I told him and he grunted.

I decided that I would like some fresh air and announced my intention of going out. Neither the Professor nor the Chief Inspector had any objections to raise. I set out. I merely intended to walk round the Heath to get my brain clear, but when I got to Pond Street[157] I decided that I would go to Mecklenburgh Square and I hopped on to a 24 bus which was standing waiting.

Things appeared to be very much as usual at Roger's. No one seemed to be deeply in mourning for Arthur Loftus. The regrets for his death were banal and unfelt. If it had not been indecent I felt that quite a number of the habitués of Roger's house would have been hanging out flags. I had the feeling that the opinion of the house was very much in line with the opinion of the chap who wrote the epitaph on Frederick, Prince of Wales:

... But since it's only poor Fred
Who was alive and is dead,
There's no more to be said.

Mary was looking as beautiful as I had ever seen her look. More beautiful, perhaps. I wouldn't know. She always seemed to me to be more beautiful every time I saw her.

"Oh hullo, Max darling," she said, and this time the "darling" had a little expression in it, "It is nice of you to come round to see me."

I pointed out, in a rather involved and tongue-tied speech, that I would travel to the moon and back to see her. She smiled. I could have turned cart-wheels down the middle of the room, or stood on my head and waved my legs. Instead I contented myself with inviting her out to lunch with me.

She hesitated for a moment and I was sadly afraid that she was about to say that she had a previous engagement. Then she smiled again and said

157 Pond Street is in Hampstead and is where George Orwell (1903-1950) stayed while working in Booklover's Corner, a secondhand bookshop.

she'd be delighted to lunch with me. I hoped this did not mean that all the others were also going to lunch with me.

It was all right. I was to have Mary to myself. There was about an hour before it was time for lunch so we all drifted round to *The Lamb* to have a drink.

Douglas Newsome seemed to be full of alcoholic remorse and a hangover. He edged up to me at the bar.

"I say, Max," his voice was eagerly apologetic, "I hope I didn't make a terrible nuisance of myself last night? I was a bit drunk and was not feeling too bright and sometimes drink takes me that way."

I assured him that I had no objections personally about his way of life or his behaviour when drunk. He pressed the subject.

"Of course," he went on, "I can't have been as drunk as all that, for I gather I only recited short passages of gloom. When I'm really drunk I can go all the way through *Macbeth*, doing all the parts, or I might have started on Flecker's *Hassan*.[158] I remember getting kicked out of Henekey's[159] in High Holborn for reciting the whole of Hassan to myself. It was funny, because I thought I was only doing it in my head, but it turned out that I was humming Delius's[160] music and doing it at the top of my voice. Really, you see," his tone was confidential, "I should not drink at all. I haven't got a strong head and I sometimes do the most frightful things when I've had a drink or two. The trouble is that I do those things and then forget all about them. They only come back to me when I'm drunk again. For a while I used to try and make notes of the terrible things I did when drunk, but I found that reading them over when I was sober was a bit too much, so I gave it up."

He took a small swallow of his beer. Something seemed to be worrying him. He stood on one foot and then on the other, curling his unused leg round the other.

"You see, Max," he continued, "I don't know that I'm not to blame for last night. If I hadn't been drunk and hadn't seen that clock pointing to

158 *Hassan: The Story of Hassan of Baghdad and How He Came to Make the Golden Journey to Samarkand* was one of two plays written by James Elroy Flecker (1884-1915).

159 Henekey's were wine and brandy merchants, established in 1695, who had a chain of free houses which were eventually acquired by Whitbreads.

160 Frederick Theodore Albert Delius (1862-1934) wrote the incidental music for *Hassan*, which ran for 281 performances at His Majesty's Theatre.

a quarter to twelve, that damn fool snatch of Beddoes would never have occurred to me and Arthur would not have been off his balance when the crowd moved. He wouldn't have fallen over in front of the train if I had not been so silly."

"Look here, Douglas," I said as sternly as I could, "It's no use your trying to persuade yourself that you are to blame for last night's business. Neither the Chief Inspector nor Professor Stubbs believe it was an accident. Either Arthur threw himself under the train, for some reason best known to himself, or he was pushed. A very weak shove delivered at exactly the right moment and in the right direction, would have been enough to tip him off the platform. You must remember that the platform was crowded and that we were pushing backwards to try and prevent being shoved over the edge ourselves. Well if someone gave Arthur a push sideways he would be off his balance and would have gone over the edge exactly as he did. I don't believe that your interlude with the clock did any more then make it easier for the murderer to deliver that push unobserved. And, at a guess, I'd say that even if we all had been looking the other way we'd have been watching the train coming into the station and so would not have seen the murderer giving it. I don't think that you can blame yourself at all for what happened."

"Yes, Max," Douglas was meekly agreeable. He edged a bit closer to me and looked round at the others. Roger and Harold and Mary were chatting together and Alec Dolittle was scribbling in his notebook. Douglas dropped his voice, "You know it isn't a nice thought that. One of us is a murderer and may choose another one as a victim at any time." He shivered expressively. "You don't think that Arthur could have murdered Stella and then committed suicide? He loathed her, you know, and would have gone out of his way to hurt her. Then you see he might have fancied that the police were on his trail and that he was bound to be caught. If he felt like that he might well have committed suicide, and, knowing Arthur, I'd say that once he'd made up his mind to kill himself, he would be sure to do it in a spectacular way and in a way that would cause as much trouble as possible to other people. He wasn't the sort of a man who'd leave a note explaining why he was doing it. He'd laugh at the idea of causing trouble by his death. You see," Douglas was very simple and direct, "I didn't like the man. I couldn't stand him at any price."

There did not seem to be much future in trying to persuade Douglas that it seemed improbable that Arthur was the murderer, so I contented myself with saying that I would pass on his opinion to the Professor and the Chief Inspector when I saw them. This seemed to relieve his mind and we wandered across to the others.

Alec Dolittle looked up. His eyes were watery with weariness and there were red rims to them and greyish bags beneath them. He looked very tired.

"What are you up to?" I asked politely, more for the sake of making conversation than from any real desire to know. He looked at me as if half ashamed of himself.

"Well," he said slowly, "I feel the most frightful ghoul, but there it is. The thing is I'm a journalist and I have to make money somehow – even out of my friends' misfortunes. One of the papers asked me if I could do a story on how death haunts Roger's house, and so I've got to do it. I asked Roger and he said he didn't mind."

He looked up at Roger who seemed to have caught the drift of the conversation.

"Good Lord, no," he said, wiping his hair back from his forehead, "I can see that some newspaper was bound to pick on us and I'd much rather the story was written by Alec than by some stranger. At least Alec will know how much to say and will try and not hurt anyone, but if we got an ordinary reporter he'd be sure to make our lives hell. Not that they aren't hell anyway."

"And this is hell," intoned Douglas, "Nor am I out of it."

"Shut up, Douglas," said Mary, "Don't you think we've had enough of your damned quotations?"

"Sorry," Douglas looked really apologetic and sat down and buried his face in his beer. He came up for air and looked round the company.

"I really am frightfully sorry," he said, "but the trouble is that this quotation bug has bitten me and I can hardly keep my mind off it. Whenever anyone says anything I immediately think of a quotation to fit it."

"You should take a job making cross-word puzzles," Harold spoke unexpectedly, "that's where quotations should he kept. They are a damned nuisance and are an excuse for avoiding intelligent remarks."

Everybody, and not least Douglas, seemed to be surprised by this sudden outburst on the part of Harold. Douglas looked doubly apologetic.

I looked at my watch and realised that it was time I took Mary off to lunch. I managed to extract her from the rest of the party. It was rather like pulling one sheaf out of a stack – the rest showed some inclination to follow. I wasn't rude but I was quite firm. I wanted, for a change, to have Mary to myself. I didn't want to have a repetition of the previous evening. I was in luck and got a taxi outside the pub. The driver was just getting into it after having his lunch in a little café on the other side of the road.

We went to *The Gargoyle*.

CHAPTER FOURTEEN

SUSPICION ON A WHEEL

As LUNCHES go it was a success. My only trouble was that I seemed to be able to get just so far with Mary and no farther. Just as I was about to say something that seemed of real importance, to me, she managed, it seemed to me wilfully, to turn aside the remark with some triviality, about some theatrical personage, or about the mirrors round the walls of the club.

But, be that as it may, I felt the whale of a lot happier when we had finished lunch and I had to go back to the Professor. I felt that I could stand up to any eccentricity he might produce from his most eccentric brain.

I did not make much noise on my arrival and when I opened the door of the old man's room I saw him lying in his chair with his mouth slightly agape and his eyes closed. He seems to have some sixth sense that tells him he's being watched. He sat up abruptly and glared at me, feeling for his pipe.

"Hullo," I said cheerfully, "Having a nap?"

He was loudly indignant. "I was not havin' a nap," he howled, "I was cogitatin'. How often ha' I got to tell ye that I think clearer wi' me eyes closed? Bah!"

Being on top of the world, I did not desire to start bickering, so I apologised humbly and asked him how he was getting on.

He glowered beneath a wrinkled forehead. "I'm gettin' on fine, thank 'ee, an' it's no thanks to ye that I am. I bin tryin' to work out reasons for the murders an' I think I'm beginnin' to get somewhere."

"Come on," I said, "give." But he shook his head heavily and said nothing for a moment. I did not return to the attack. I was beginning to learn sense when I saw him like that. I held my tongue and sat down at my table and pulled my papers towards me.

It was difficult to concentrate but I managed to get something down on paper. As I was turning over my various notes I found that a couple of loose pages from the *British Medical Journal*[161] had wandered in among them. These consisted of an article on *Poisoning by Amanita Phalloides*, by Doctors Jal Dubash and Donald Teare. The article was dated January 12, 1946, so it seemed to me that it was probably the most up-to-date stuff on the subject. I read it through carefully and found it very interesting, but the trouble was that it did not seem to give me any hint in the way of solving *who* had done it. We already knew *how*, but we did not know *who* or *why*.

Being a chap who likes a quiet life and who does not like seeing his friends involved in unpleasantness, it occurred to me that the obvious solution was that Arthur Loftus had murdered Stella Mortimer and had then committed suicide. I started to work out a nice programme to prove this. Here is what I wrote:

ARTHUR LOFTUS as murderer. He did not like Stella. Query? Had he had an affair with her and was he roused to feelings of jealousy by the sight of her and Roger? Answer: damned doubtful; he seemed to me a cold fish. Query? Is there a hidden motive? Answer: it looks like it.

Opportunity: He had as much opportunity and more than anyone else in the house or among those who had been in a position to gather mushrooms. He could have picked the *Amanita* when he was out with Mary and Stella and could have brought them back to town with him. He was hanging about the kitchen during the cooking and could easily have slipped the Death Cap into Stella's portion of mushrooms on toast. The article in the *B.M.J.* says that "When fresh this fungus is odourless and tasteless." That would have solved the question of why Stella had not noticed it. And, about the question of its usual greenness, the same article says, "It must be remembered that there are aberrant forms of the fungus; the colour may range from pure white to yellow." Thinking of that I realised that, if the murderer had peeled off the volva, and no one had noticed the white gills, the *Amanita phalloides* might very well have passed as a mushroom after being cooked.

Looking through the article again, one notes that there have been 21 cases in the last 15 years of which 14 have proved fatal. The murderer was obviously not familiar with this article, or he would have not risked only a 66% certainty. The King Penguin, on the other hand, suggests a much higher rate of fatality. Query? Was the information derived from that book? Anyone familiar with the position in France would have deemed *Amanita*

161 The *British Medical Journal* started life in 1840 as the *Provincial Medical and Surgical Journal*.

phalloides pretty dangerous. The *B.M.J.* says "The position was so serious in France that in 1925 a law was enacted providing that there should be inspectors at all market towns, to pass mushrooms as fit for human consumption. The efficacy of this law can be judged by the fact that in 1930 the mushroom inspector at Fougères died of fungus poisoning." Tough on the mushroom inspector, but it only goes to show how easily the poisonous *Amanita* can be confused with the harmless *Psalliota campestris* or field mushroom.

Well, then, supposing that Arthur had had some reason for wishing to kill Stella and had worked out the almost foolproof method, and had carried it out successfully, it must have been an awful shock when Douglas came out of his drunken stupor and remembered that he and Stella had only eaten cultivated mushrooms and that she could not have been poisoned by these.

Putting myself in his position, I realise that, once the discovery had been made that my insoluble murder was recognised as murder and not as a simple and regrettable accident, I'd begin wondering what people knew and I might fancy that an innocent remark was a hint from someone that they knew more than was healthy for me. In that case I do not think I would commit suicide, but then I'm not Arthur Loftus.

Supposing that he was a character of suicidal tendencies; the discovery that there was suspicion about, might be quite enough to drive him to kill himself. It would have been in keeping for Arthur to kill himself and leave no indication of his having done so – leaving it for others to sort out whether he had been murdered or whether it was an accident.

Query? The causes of both deaths could not have been accidents? Here the answer seems, definitely, to be NO! ! !

I read through the bit of paper on which I had made these notes. They did not seem to make much sense. I crumpled the paper and threw it towards the waste-paper basket.

It was a damned bad shot. I missed the basket by a couple of feet. The old man leaned over and picked up the ball. He straightened it out, rubbing out the creases with the side of his hand. He placed his glasses right upon his nose and started to read. I could see no reason why he should not read what I had written, so I held my peace. He grumbled in an undertone to himself as he made his way through the sprawl of my hand-writing. He always grumbles like that whenever he has to read anything which I've written. His own hand is as neat as an Italian hand of the sixteenth century, and as legible.

I fiddled with my pen while he read. I felt that any moment he might look up and start tearing holes in my argument, and I was already preparing to be defensive. I had only been trying to get things straight in my own mind, and what I had written was for my eyes and brains alone – not meant to be examined destructively by anyone else.

As he turned to me, the Professor's glasses began to slide down his blunt nose. He peered at me through the gap between the steel rims and his bushy eyebrows.

"Ye got it almost all there," he remarked in a deep voice, "but ye can't see the answer. I'm workin' towards that an' I don't quite know where it'll lead me, an' I can't say I like where it points at the moment. Ye might try all the others in the part o' Arthur Loftus an' see where that gets ye. I bin doin' that, in me mind, an' I know where it gets me."

This did not seem to elucidate anything and I said so. The Professor suddenly changed the subject.

"D'ye know," he announced suddenly, with the air of one dropping an atomic bomb, "that if ye weren't me assistant an' if the worthy Bishop didn't know ye, that ye might be havin' an unpleasant time at the moment?"

"No," I said, truthfully. I had not the slightest idea what he was getting at. My conscience was as clear as that of a week-old baby.

"Ho," the Professor chortled, "We got a witness who thinks ye shoved Arthur Loftus off the edge o' the platform."

"Good God," I said, frankly astonished, "who the hell would think that? I'd never have dreamed of helping the late lamented to his everlasting bourne. I'd have been too frightened of the things you would do in your efforts to promote justice and your own fair fame."

If I hadn't been so surprised, I might have been angry. But the idea that I should have pushed Arthur under the train was so fantastic that I could hardly take it in. It was the sort of thing which no one in their senses could have believed. "Who said that?"

"So ye're surprised, eh?" the old man was gleeful, "I just bin waitin' for someone to suggest that either you or I ha' bin committin' murders to gi' ourselves somethin' to do. Well, it was an unbiased witness all right. An old bird who lives in Somers Town[162] and who thought that you were an uncommon noisy set. I think she was kinda tired. But she says that just as

162 Somers Town was an area built up from about 1786 on land owned by Lord Somers.

the train came in ye gave a kind of hitch and that ye might ha' bin edgin' Arthur on to the edge."

"Hell, dammit," I said, faintly crossly, "I couldn't have done it. Mary was hanging on to my arm and I was watching Douglas. We were being pushed around by the crowd behind us and no doubt I staggered occasionally in my efforts to remain upright. If we had remained like ramrods we'd all have been pushed off the edge of the platform. You know yourself how you can't remain absolutely still in a heaving crowd. But for the idea that I gave Arthur the shove that sent him under the train – why that's the dottiest idea I've heard for a long time. I must admit that I didn't like him, I don't think anyone did, but at the same time I'd never have bothered to murder him. He didn't come near enough to my sort of world. So far as I was concerned, he was the sort of chap whom I wouldn't go out of my way to meet, and if I did have to meet him, I would make my stay in his company as short as possible. I would have avoided him, but not murdered him. He wasn't worth the trouble!"

The old man seemed to be vastly amused. His bulk shook with laughter which could not, by any standards, have been described as silent.

"Ho, ho," he hooted. I glared at him.

"Stop making a noise like Billy Bunter," I snapped, "and tell me where you got this fantastic idea!"

Professor Stubbs whipped a large violently coloured bandana out of his pocket and ostentatiously dried the tears of his eyes. I must have looked about as sour as an unripe crab-apple.

"I'm sorry, Max," he said at last, and his voice was genuinely humble, "I didn't mean to hurt yer feelin's. I just thought ye ought to know that ye'd bin included in the runnin' for the hempen noose. I thought it might amuse ye. Ye know that neither the Chief Inspector or meself 'ud take a thin' like that seriously. We'd know that there was some kinda mistake, but it was odd that the only person who seemed to move at the right time was ye. That is, o' course, so far as the old woman knows. She seems honest enough, for she admits that there was the devil o' a crush on the platform an' that she was only watchin' ye. One o' the disadvantages o' bein' like the bean-stalk, Max, is that ye're so dam' obvious in a crowd. Ye can see over the heads o' the others, but they are also watchin' ye all the time, envyin' ye yer height on occasions when there's anythin' to see, and usin' ye as a kinda landmark when there ain't."

I could see that the Professor was right. I have often noticed in a crowd that I am very conspicuous – the trouble being that I am abnormally tall, as thin as a Maypole and that the whole is topped off with a face that looks as though someone had started to make an extra gargoyle for Notre Dame and had got bored with the idea half way through.

All the same, I didn't like the idea that my physical peculiarities had marked me down as a possible for the murder team. I said as much, in a voice full of complaint and the horror of being misunderstood.

"Well, Max," the Professor was placatory, "ye got nothin' to worry about this time. Ye're cleared o' all complicity in the death o' Stella Mortimer an' I don't think that even the Bishop could think ye're startin' murderin' people for the fun o' it. But ye'd better let this be a lesson to ye, not to go mixin' yerself where murders happen. Choose yer friends more carefully in future."

I was indignant, but I might as well have gone out and been indignant to a saxifrage in the garden. I blew up this way and that and would have destroyed anyone of less bulk than the old man. To think that I was being accused of mixing with murders! It was just my bad luck that they happened when I was around. If it had been Professor Stubbs, now, I would not have been the least surprised to hear that battle, murder and sudden death were following him round like a shadow. He liked these sort of things, but me, hell I was all for a quiet life. I had wanted a quiet life, and had I found it? No! I announced my decision of taking a holiday as soon as the case was cleared up. I announced it with decision and without equivocation.

Professor Stubbs beamed at me. Usually he would have answered my brick-bats with his heavy artillery, but this afternoon he just looked benevolent.

"Right you are, Max boy," he said surprisingly mildly, "ye have yer short holiday after we wind this dam' affair up an' put it away on the shelf. Ye can take yer holiday an' I promise ye I'll do me best not to muddle up things till ye get back. I'm thinkin' ye need a break."

This was very unusual. As a rule when I said I wanted my long-promised and much overdue holiday the old man found some reason why I should postpone it for a week or two, and then something would break and I wouldn't get it after all. Frankly I was getting a little tired of the mirage of my holiday. It's not that Professor Stubbs does not want me to have a rest; he's always urging me to go away for a short holiday, but somehow it never comes off. I hoped I'd have better luck this time.

It took the Professor some time to calm me down. I would not say that I was of a very excitable nature, but there's something about the old man that gets under my skin, so I feel I've got a death-watch beetle in my bones.

Once I was calmed down, however, Professor Stubbs took care not to rouse me again and we spent the rest of the afternoon trying to get some order into his notes on the *History of Botany*. I may say that the Augean stable[163] has nothing on the Professor's work-table. I wrestled with the notes, typing and filing and cross-indexing them until it was dark.

The old man rose heavily from the chair and lumbered across to the beer-barrel. He drew a quart for himself and a pint for me. I do pretty well in the way of thirsts but I can't hold a dry water-hole to the old man. When I suggest that he drinks too much he scowls and points out that he dehydrates faster than most people and that he needs more liquid to keep him going. This seems to be true, for I've seen him drinking tea and coffee in the same sort of measure that he uses for beer.

When we'd had our drink he looked up at me. "We got company to-night," he observed airily.

"Who is it?" I was suspicious. The old man has a habit of passing seemingly innocent remarks like this and then letting it out that he has invited a murderer or a burglar to dinner. He laughed gustily.

"Ye needn't worry," he said, "it's an old friend of yours. The Chief Inspector. He thought he would come round and see if we could get any place by millin' over the facts between the stones o' our minds."

"Oh," I said. I wasn't pleased. "I hope that he won't try and be funny about the old girl who saw me shoving Arthur Loftus off the platform. If he does, I won't be answerable for what I say."

The Chief Inspector did try and be funny. He made jokes which were in the worst of taste about my breakfast on the morning of execution. He admitted that he was surprised that I had sunk to murder, but then he went on to deliver a homily which he had stolen from Professor Stubbs. This deals with the matter of murder being the abnormal action of a normal person rather than the normal action of an abnormal one.

Queen Victoria must have shaken the Royal Chambers with laughter compared with my attitude. I was so unamused that I might have been

163 The fifth labour of Heracles was the cleaning of the Augean stables, an apparently impossible task as they contained 1000 cattle and had not been cleaned for 30 years.

frozen in an ice-box all the way from the Argentine. After a while my presence started filtering through the Chief Inspector's layers of warming fat, and even he started to realise that he was not making me laugh.

He looked at me through half-closed eyelids. He seemed rather more than half-asleep. Where a moment before he had been full of life and some laughter, he now appeared to be bored and full of sorrows. I was not in the least sympathetic. I showed my feelings in my attitude of withdrawal from his puerile jokes.

"Am I putting my foot in it, Max?" he asked sleepily, "if I am I'm sorry. I forgot you've probably had nothing else from John Stubbs all afternoon. Am I forgiven?"

There didn't seem to be anything else I could do, so I said that he was as gracefully as I could. After all it was the old man who had flogged that horse to death, so there was no use in my holding the crime against the Chief Inspector. He was not to blame. The report had come in and he'd had to kill it. I should, I supposed, be glad he had not been unpleasant but had only tried to be funny.

"Um," the Professor grunted, "I think Max has had enough o' the subject, but before we finish it, we'd better make certain that he's quite sure that no one gave him a shove which might ha' brought him up against Arthur Loftus hard enough to push him over, eh, Max?"

"Well, of course," I began slowly, "I'd rather a lot to drink during the course of the evening. We all had. And I don't think that Arthur was any steadier on his pins than the rest of us, so even a fairly weak shoulder charge like those in soccer *might* have thrown him off his balance. I don't, myself, remember giving him a shove. I remember bumping Mary, as she was holding on to my arm, but I don't think I could have hit Arthur hard enough to push him over. You must remember that we were all in a sort of huddle, and that none of us were quite sober, and you may see that it is quite impossible for any one of us to swear that we did not knock against Arthur, by accident, and push him over. You know, Bishop, that there is the odd chance that Arthur's death was an accident. Even though all the people concerned in Stella's death were there, there is no reason to think that anyone feared Arthur enough to kill him. It might have been an accident, mightn't it?"

"No," the Chief Inspector was sleepy, "I don't believe in fairy-tales, and I don't believe that the one man who knew something was the man who was killed by accident. I can't believe it. These things *may* happen, but they happen damned rarely in my experience. What do you say, John?"

This was the sort of invitation that the Professor can never withstand. It is an invitation for him to take the floor and lay down the law.

"Ha," he said brightly, coming up from the depths of his beer, "I agree wi' ye, Reggie. If I was to start believin' in every accident that was o' use to a murderer, before I knew where I was I'd be doubtin' the validity o' experimental proof an' then where would I be? I'll tell ye. Back where I was when I was fifteen an' believed everythin' I was told wi'out tryin' to work it out for meself. I just don't see Loftus fallin' under a train to oblige someone whom he knew too much about. I'm not sayin', mark ye, that such things don't happen – for they do. Just you look at the way that young Max, there, attracts murder. But I'm sayin' that it's bad enough to ha' one person around to whom things are always happenin' wi'out askin' me to believe that there can be two oddities on an underground platform at the same time. That's askin' too much from me. If Arthur Loftus had met his death under the same circumstances an' Max had not bin there, I might ha' bin willin' to believe that it was an accident, but ye can't ask me to swallow both Max's presence an' an accident. That 'ud be too much, much too much, in fact."

He buried his face, or as much of it as he could squeeze into the pot, in his beer and I thought he had finished. But not him. He was just taking some refreshment before continuing.

"It still seems to me," he grumbled, "that we got to concentrate on the murder o' Stella Mortimer before we can get at the murderer o' Arthur Loftus. The murder o' Loftus is a kinda bud on the tree o' the murder o' the girl. If we can find out who murdered her, we'll know who killed Loftus. I'm not, o' course, sayin' that this wouldn't work in reverse, but it seems to me that if the best witnesses can do is to point to Max as the killer o' Loftus, we're not likely to get a line from that. No, Reggie, if we can find who killed Stella Mortimer, an' why, we'll ha' the key to the whole affair. An' one o' the points ye mustn't forget is that if the affair had passed as an accident Loftus 'ud never ha' bin in danger. It was only when it was suggested that it was a murder that he became dangerous. He must ha' known somethin'. An' it must ha' bin somethin' which the murderer knew was dangerous – as soon as it became known that the girl's death was not accidental."

The Chief Inspector looked about as pleased as a child who has been offered a dose of castor-oil, without anything to disguise the taste.

"That's all very well," he said peevishly and wearily, "it's all very well for you to theorise away like that, John. You don't need to prove anything, nor do you need to appear in court in support of your theories. It's quite likely that there was something which was known to Loftus and which was consequently of danger to the murderer. But tell me what it was? Loftus is dead and I must say I don't see the murderer coming along quietly and saying, 'Look here, I murdered Loftus because he knew so-and-so about me.' No, no, John, the trouble with you is that you are as pleased with an idea as you are with proof."

"An' what the thunderin' such-an'-such," the old man demanded aggressively, "d'ye think ye mean by that? Who's not interested in proof? Me? Bah, I say an' bah again! I'm a blinkin' scientist an' me whole life's spent in search o' proof, an' ye ha' the nerve to sit there lookin' like a plump eunuch cat an' tell me I'm not interested in proof. O' course, I'm interested in proof – I'm more interested in that than in anythin' else – but ye'd never start lookin' for the proof if ye didn't think o' somethin' that ye wanted to prove first. Ye don't just start out doin' experiments in the hope that somethin' will come o' them – no, man, no, ye starts out wi' an idea in yer head an' ye want to find out if it is so, or if it ain't. O' course, the notion o' havin' an' idea in yer head may be kinda strange to ye, for so far as I can see ye got nothin' in yer head but stuffin', to allow it to stand up to the pressure o' the atmosphere wi'out collapsin'."

The Bishop, as bland as a patent drink for nursing mothers, ignored this sally at the contents of his skull. He took an appreciative sip of the brandy with which the Professor had supplied him.

"It's no use losing your rag, John," he remarked, looking at the inch of ash on his cigar, "that won't make things any clearer. If you could give me some suggestions as to *what* Loftus might have known that made him dangerous, I'll be grateful for them, and I will try to find proof of your correctness or inaccuracy for you."

"Pfff," the Professor blew noisily between his lips, "how d'ye expect me to know? I don't know nuffin. I'm Brer Rabbit an' lie low an' say nuffin. I ain't got the resources o' the police at me command. All I got is Max, here, an' as likely as not he's buzzin' off in pursuit o' a girl when I'm wantin' him."

I flushed angrily. I was beginning to feel annoyed by the way the old man referred to my affection for Mary as if I was in the habit of dashing after every girl I saw with a lustful expression on my face. I might have said something, but instead I took a pull at my beer.

"Ye know," the old man sounded faintly odd to me, "that it might pay ye to look into young Newsome. He seems to be around too much at the right time, an' he certainly distracted attention o' those on the platform by his outburst from Beddoes."

"But," I began, "you told me that you thought Douglas's mind was only running on quotations which dealt with death, and that his remark at that moment was quite fortuitous – produced by the time of the clock."

"Uhhuh," the old man nodded, "I did think that for a moment an' it's more than likely that it's true, but since the Chief Inspector wants somethin' to prove I'm handin' him Douglas. O' course, if he is guilty I dunno what game he's playin', for after all he drew our attention to the fact that Stella Mortimer had bin eatin' cultivated mushrooms an' not some o' those gathered in the field. But, ye got to remember that on both occasions when there was a death he was in a position to ha' caused them. An' in the case o' Loftus he drew all attention to the clock an' away from the arrivin' train."

"I don't believe he could have done it," I replied, "I was quite close to him and I was watching him as much as I was watching the clock. He had been behaving very oddly all evening – that is his behaviour would have been odd in anyone else, but with Douglas one never knows – he's as unpredictable as the English climate. I was studying him as he is the sort of unbalanced creature who interests me – he is unbalanced about everything except his work, and there his behaviour is all that you could ask of him. I feel morally certain that, if he had given Loftus a sudden shove, I'd have noticed it."

"Bah!" the old man was rude, "ye were as drunk as a coot. I could see it in yer eyes when ye came in. The fright had pulled ye together, but ye weren't sober. Ye'd never ha' passed a police drivin' test."

I got up and went in search of some cigarettes. It seemed more politic to avoid a direct row with the old man. Let him be as testy as he liked, I would set him an example of good humour.

When I got back into the room he was laying down the law to the Chief Inspector.

"Uhhuh," he was saying, "well, by this time ye should know me method o' approach to the case. I got certain things I do in me mind an' then I see what'll happen if I try 'em out. First o' all, an' naturally, I try everyone connected wi' the case in the part o' murderer an' it usually comes round to it that one or two fit the part better than the rest. Now when I got me list down to that number, say two or three, I then start thinkin' o' each o' 'em as the victim an' the victim as murderer. The trouble is ye got to know the hell o' a lot about each o' the characters involved afore ye can get anythin' out o' this system. Now in this dam' case the trouble is that I don't know enough about Stella Mortimer. I want to find out a bit more about that girl. Once I done that I can get things straight in me mind."

It seemed to me that the rest of the evening was to be devoted to a theoretical approach to murder, with everyone, not excluding myself, in the part of first, murderer, and then victim. I really did not see why I should sit up half the night listening to things I had already heard or of which, knowing Professor Stubb's methods, I had thought. Anyhow, I told myself, I felt very tired. I made my apologies and went to bed.

CHAPTER FIFTEEN

ONE BY ONE

I THOUGHT I was up pretty early in the morning. I usually beat the Professor to it by a good ten minutes, but when I got up I found a note pinned to the door of the dining-room: "Had breakfast – gone to country – back this evening."

I thought that it was a poor show on the part of the old man to go cavorting around the country without me, but there was nothing I could do about it. Anyhow, I was able to read *The Times* in comfort, without either interruptions or demands for the piece I was reading.

Having breakfast alone certainly had other compensations. There was no bickering. I could reach out and get as much coffee as I wanted without the fear of finding that the old man had drained the pot in his efforts to rehydrate himself.

All the same, when I had drained the pot myself and had finished a generous double ration of toast and Oxford marmalade, I had to admit that I felt pretty lost without the Professor around. I wondered what kind of mischief he was engaged upon, and how much extra work by myself would be required to disentangle him from any mess he succeeded in getting into. I am not what you might call sanguine about the Professor when he goes on the loose. Only too often I've been rung up by him asking me to bring him some money or to send an engineer to Swindon to repair his car which has chosen to go wrong in that Mecca of mechanics.[164] One of the old man's pet theories is that he is a natural mechanic himself. He certainly has a liking for gadgets of all kinds, but he has no more idea of what makes them go than a snake has of how to rumba.

I wandered through into the workroom and picked up a number of

164 Swindon was the site of the Great Western Railway's works which at their height employed 14,000 men and were still producing 60 locomotives a year at the time of the story.

Nature. Of course, with the sort of luck that was with me, it was bound to be the number published in 1944 with an article by J. Ramsbottom on the subject of poisonous fungi.[165] It seemed to me that I would never get away from the subject. I almost felt that I could never look a mushroom in the face again, and this would have been unfortunate as mushrooms are a delicacy I'm pretty fond of.

The way things were I knew I could not settle down to do any serious work on my own subject. It was then that I had a bright idea. If the old man could play detective, why shouldn't I? I had not, of course, the same mental equipment, but then the old man was often wrong before he was right, so maybe I could, at least, do a bit of his being wrong for him and save him the waste of time.

I sat and contemplated my mind. Although I did not wish to make either of them into the murderer, it seemed to me that I should begin the day by trying to find out a bit more about Douglas Newsome and Alec Dolittle. I already knew quite a lot about Douglas, but I didn't know what his dreams were or what his private personal life was like. I only knew him as a public figure, rather too full of drink.

As for Alec Dolittle – well, he was a fairly familiar figure. The drunken and comparatively unsuccessful journalist, living from day to day and from one small scoop to another. It hardly seemed likely, though, that he would have started a career as a murderer just to supply himself with stuff of news value. That would be going a bit too far. Even Edgar Wallace[166] had never supplied a murderer with a motive as flimsy as that. I did not know what I could expect to find out about Alec Dolittle, but I thought I would make a start in my career as understudy to the great detective, a sort of Sexton Blake's Tinker rather than a Sherlock Holmes's Watson. I was damned if I would be Watson. I sometimes admit to myself that I am fonder of the old man than he knows, but I'd never let him see it, nor would I blind myself to his faults, which are multitudinous and magnificent.

I left the house wrapped in my overcoat and an air of mystery.[167] I told

---

165 Ramsbottom's article was titled *Fungi and Modern Affairs*, and appeared in the issue dated 27th May 1944.

166 Edgar Wallace (1875-1932) was a prolific writer, producing over 175 novels and numerous articles for newspapers and journals. His first thriller was *Four Just Men*, published through his own publishing company, Tallis Press, in 1905.

167 An example of syllepsis, or semantic zeugma, similar to one used in Chapter 19 of *Take Thee a Sharp Knife*.

Mrs. Farley that I did not expect to be in for lunch and asked her if the old man had left any indication as to when he might be expected home. She shook her head. Her attitude to the Professor is that of one who understands all and is therefore able to forgive it. She must be a most remarkable woman to have put up with his foibles and untidiness for all these years without so much as a grumble. I don't know what she says to her husband about the Professor, but I must say that, even when he has forgotten a perfect lunch, I have never heard Mrs. Farley murmur.

Since I was to play detective, I thought I might as well begin at the scene of the crime, particularly as all the suspects were still on that scene. I wandered down to the bus stop, letting my steps wander round by the ponds to see if any of the perennial fishermen had caught anything. They had not caught anything, but as they rarely do, I could hardly count that as a bad omen for my outing.

It was a lovely day. I must admit that I envied the Professor his outing to the country. I wished I was going to Linton or down into Hampshire.

Roger opened the door of his house to me himself.

"Hullo, Max," he said cheerfully, "you're becoming quite a regular here aren't you?"

He was carrying a few rather bedraggled oil brushes in his hand and, realising that I had interrupted his work, I looked up sharply to see if there was any rebuke hidden in his words. There was not. He seemed to be genuinely pleased that I had arrived. I followed him into his painting room.

"I was just going to have a cup of coffee," he said, kicking a gurgling electric kettle as he passed it, "will you have a cup?"

I said I would and he laid down his brushes. I looked at the little painting propped up on the easel. It looked like so many other paintings by Roger that I had seen – a mixture of Torres García and Paul Klee – that I could not think of anything to say. I had exhausted the possible combinations of the words "delicate", "expressive" and "exquisite". It was fortunate that this did not seem to matter. Roger showed no desire to hear me voice an opinion. This may have been due to his modesty about his own work, or else just to the fact that he considered that I knew nothing about painting and had no right to have an opinion. I didn't know and I didn't care.

Sitting on the edge of the couch, sipping strong hot coffee, I made an effort to open my campaign as the detective.

"I say, Roger," I said, rather diffidently, for the subject was not too easy to broach, "you know that Professor Stubbs is rather interested in the matter of Stella's death?"

Roger's face was crossed by a grimace, as though he had just bitten on a bone in his sausage. "Yes, I know," he replied, absently, as though he was not thinking of Professor Stubbs at all, but was remembering the dead girl who had been killed under his roof.

"I'm sorry," I went on, "if I cause you any pain by going on about this subject, but you know that the police will never let it rest and it is only fair, for the sake of the innocent, that the guilty should be rooted out and removed."

To this string of platitudes Roger made no answer. He just nodded his head like one of these Chinese mandarins in an old fashioned tea-shop window. The nod expressed nothing, neither approval nor disapproval of my attitude.

"The point that gets me, Roger," I began again, "is that – now that Arthur is no longer here – I like everyone in this house and I do not wish to believe that any one would have been guilty of killing Stella in that cruel and beastly fashion. She must have suffered a great deal."

"She did." Roger was sharp and his voice was bitter. "If I could lay my hands on the person who was responsible for Stella's death I think I would strangle them. I would do it slowly and let them recover at short intervals."

This outburst faintly surprised me till I remembered that Roger had nursed Stella throughout her illness. I had only been there in short stretches and so I could hardly have realised her condition. I remembered short snatches from the descriptions of the four cases given by the two doctors in the *British Medical Journal*. They had not been pretty or pleasing.

"You see, Max," Roger went on, "since Stella's death I have thought of closing the house and going abroad for a short time. This would be a way of dispersing all the people who could possibly have been responsible for her death. On the other hand, I tell myself that I can't do that, for when everyone is still here, there is some chance that the guilty person will give himself away. I watch all the time, but I see nothing. The morning I heard that Stella had been murdered and that it was not the result of an accident I think I was slightly mad. I might have stayed that way if it hadn't been for Mary – she's been absolutely wonderful – nothing is too much trouble for her to do it and she is sympathetic without being so solicitous as to become tiresome."

I felt a faint twang of jealousy at hearing Roger describe how good Mary had been, but it passed. All along I'd thought she was the most wonderful girl in the world and here was additional evidence of the rightness of my taste. The jealousy was replaced by pleasure at hearing her praised.

"Well, Roger," I said, "you know all these people far better than I do; what do you think of each of them? Have you thought of anyone in particular who might have murdered Stella, and then, in a sudden panic, have pushed Arthur Loftus under the wheels of that train? What about young Douglas?"

Roger dug in his pockets for a cigarette, failed to find one and took one from the packet I offered him. He puffed at it slowly and fixed his eyes in the centre of a perfect smoke-ring.

"No," his voice was slow and thoughtful, "Douglas didn't do it. He had had some kind of affair with Stella, of course, but he's adult enough mentally to take the break-up of something like that in the normal way. All he would do would be to have a few drinks – he would excuse them to himself by saying that he was drowning his sorrows – then he would write a few poems about his unhappiness and finally he would forget what he was being unhappy about. The habit of unhappiness would, of course, persist for a little, but finally it would become merged into his natural melancholia and he would bury that blow like he has buried every other blow in his life, even the biggest one of being born at all. When he's tight, too, Douglas expresses a desire for blood and misery, for pain and the deepest sort of anguish, but if you examine his desire at all, you will quickly realise that it is a purely literary desire, fed on the *Revenger's Tragedy* and not on *The Police Gazette*,[168] *The News of the World*[169] or American pulp-magazines. No, Max, I think you would be safe in saying that no matter how bitter he felt or whatever hidden reason he might have, Douglas would never have killed Stella – least of all in the way in which it was done. A murder by Douglas would be almost bound to resemble the last scene in *Hamlet*, and the drama would be stressed by his own dramatic exit from a world of tears. 'No,' he says, 'no, I am not Prince Hamlet nor was meant to be,' but in his

168 *The Police Gazette*, first appeared as *The Quarterly Pursuit* in 1772 and was instigated by John Fielding of the Bow Street Police Court to provide notification of wanted criminals and requests for information from other police authorities.
169 *The News of the World* ran from 1843-2011 and became, for a while, the largest selling English language newspaper in the world (over 9 million copies) based on its populist stories.

dreams I sometimes think he sees himself in the part of the tragic figure with all the world against him, but I cannot see him scheming to assert his fancied rights. I'm afraid that whoever murdered Stella it wasn't Douglas."

I was surprised to find Roger so communicative. I thought I might as well run down the list of those in the house. "How about Harold Ironside?" I asked, "Do you think that he might have murdered Stella?"

Roger shook his head slowly. "Not on your life. Harold is a large St. Bernard dog whose only purpose in life is to be kindly. He was a professional brute, you must remember, who got sick of it and who took up the activity as far removed from it as he possibly could. It was obvious that he could not be a ballet dancer, but that, I'm sure, was what he would have liked to have been. He was, as you know, very deeply in love with Stella, but I don't think she returned his feeling. Like all of us," Roger's voice was slightly ashamed as if he was recalling his own past bad temper, "Stella was very friendly with Harold and she liked him a lot. I don't believe she'd ever have married him, no matter how often he'd asked her. She was very wrapped up in her career as an actress and she was a damned good actress. It isn't as if I was personally biased when I say that. A lot of people who know far more about these things than I do are of the same opinion. It looked as though she might become one of the best actresses on the English stage. There was no one of her age who could come near her. To get back to Harold, however, I cannot believe that he murdered Stella. To be quite truthful, he is a bit too stupid to work out a murder like that and, in the second place, he could not kill by poisoning. Now, if I heard that someone had been smothered in his embraces I wouldn't be the least bit surprised," Roger gave a rather startled giggle, "but I don't believe that he would kill anyone intentionally. Even if his temper was roused he would attack from the front and not from behind. So you see that he could not be held responsible for either Stella's or Arthur's deaths. They weren't the kind of murders which he would have committed even at the last resort."

"Of course," I was tentative, "that might just be his cleverness. He might argue that as he was big and bluff and straightforward no one would suspect him of a sneaking kind of murder. It would be almost impossible to produce him in court, with his record of kindness and gentleness, and get a conviction for a mean murder. What do you think of that? Do you agree?"

Roger shook his head decisively. "No, Max, I don't. I think it is quite impossible to think of Harold as a killer. You could prove that he was with all the evidence a policeman ever dreamed of and I still wouldn't believe that he was guilty. No. Harold was almost as badly cut up over Stella's death as I was."

"Well, then," I persisted, "what do you think of the idea that Stella was killed by Arthur Loftus who then let his conscience ride him into committing suicide?"

"I've been trying," Roger spoke slowly, "to persuade myself that that was exactly what happened, but, you know, Max, I don't think that it will hold water as a solution. Arthur Loftus was the sort of spiteful mean creature who, given the provocation, real or imagined, was quite capable of trying to hurt Stella – if he was sure that by doing so he was running no personal risk. I was slowly persuading myself that he had in fact killed Stella, either intentionally or as the result of a bad joke – for we must remember that the person who gave Stella the Death Cap might have been under the impression that they would only make her sick – there might have been no murderous intention behind it. As I say, I was persuading myself that Arthur was, in fact, responsible for Stella's death, and I might have succeeded in convincing myself, but for his death. He would never in a thousand years have killed himself. He had that queer perverted pride of those who imagine that all flesh is grass but their own and that that is immortal. I don't believe that if he had been in a concentration camp and was suffering the torments of hell and had suddenly been given a flask of poison, painless poison, that he would have taken that way out. He could not have brought himself to the point of realising that there was no tomorrow for Arthur Loftus and that he had an easy and painless escape. His imagination could not grasp the idea of the negation of himself. Of course, there is the chance that his slip in front of that train was accidental, but there again, I can't believe that. He was always so careful of himself. If he had slipped he would have grabbed one of us. No, Max, Arthur Loftus was shoved under that train just as surely as you're sitting here."

I reached over and poured myself some more coffee. Roger seemed to be very certain of the things he was saying. He did not hesitate in admitting his friends' weaknesses, but, on the other hand, from these very weaknesses he built a wall of strength against anyone's suspecting them.

"All right then," I said, "we come to it. How about Alec Dolittle?"

"Ah," Roger did not seem so comfortable, "there I'm afraid you have me. I don't really know a great deal about Alec. He's always pleasant and he's usually broke and drunk. I don't suppose that anyone knows a great deal about him. He is not very communicative about himself. He tells endless stories about the various things that have happened to him in different parts of the world, but he never really casts any light on his character. He is really extraordinarily secretive for a man who talks so much about himself. It is rather as if he was building up a special façade to oppose to the winds of the world. If he talks hard enough, it would seem he argues, no one will want to find out about him. I know that he had some secret which he seemed to share with Stella, but I always supposed that it was something to do with publicity. He would write her up in the various rags for which he does paragraphs and that would help her while helping himself."

"Then," I asked bluntly, "you think it possible that Alec Dolittle killed both Stella and Arthur Loftus? Is that what you're driving at?"

"I would not like to be definite," Roger's voice belied his words, "but I'm afraid that the only possible solution that I can see is that, in fact, Alec Dolittle did the murders. As I have already shown you it is quite impossible that any of the others could have done them, and that, by a simple process of elimination, leaves Alec."

Odd, I thought, how each man discussing a murder always leaves himself out of the list of possible murderers. A small doubt was nagging in my mind. I was wondering if, after all, Roger had been as fond of Stella as he had claimed to be. Was it not possible that, having got himself into what seemed to be an impossible situation, he had suddenly thought longingly of the freedom he was to lose, and have taken a step which he immediately and desperately regretted. The idea had no sooner occurred to me than I dismissed it. After all, the people in the case were all modern people living in a modem world, and a little thing like a broken marriage was not enough to cause murders among such people. Roger had no need to give up his freedom if he did not want to do so.

"You see, Max," Roger's voice was forthright and made me ashamed of the doubt which had just hatched like a worm in my mind, "I never bothered about Stella and Alec. I admit I was for a time jealous of Harold – stupidly and blindly jealous about nothing. But I could not imagine a girl like that having anything to do with a man like him. He may be amusing at times, but that is not enough. He can be so boring when he's drunk and when he insists on telling rather obscene stories about his misadventures in Portuguese West Africa.[170] I must admit I rather liked him – he was out of the ordinary run of drunken journalists, but now that I have the feeling that somehow he is responsible for these deaths, I feel that I do not want

170 This is now Angola.

to see him. I am afraid that I might give my suspicions away and that I might warn him, and he might escape. You know, Max, I would never have said I was a vindictive person, but when I remember Stella's face as she lay there, wracked with pain, I cannot but wish to hurt the person responsible even more."

"You have nothing in the way of evidence, I suppose," I said, "that will serve to back up your suspicions? Nothing but your feeling that by eliminating the others you have picked on the guilty person?"

"No," said Roger slowly, "I'm afraid I have nothing. You see I am not a policeman and I do not know what constitutes evidence. I have the feeling that I am right in my accusation and that there was something which I did not understand between Alec and Stella, but that is all."

CHAPTER SIXTEEN

AROUND IN THE MORNING

I SPENT the rest of the day in wandering among the bookshops, seeing what I could find. I found plenty – far more than I really could afford. I think book-buying is a disease like diabetes – lack of money is an insulin which holds it in check, but it can't be cured. I really went on the burst and bought the whole of R. T. Gunther's[171] *Early Science in Oxford*[172], fourteen volumes of it. I took a taxi back to Hampstead, wondering rather gloomily where I hoped to house it; the shelves in my rooms have ceased being bookshelves and have become book-hammocks, sagging in the middle with the weight of the burden they are expected to bear.[173]

Professor Stubbs had not yet returned. I wondered more than ever what kind of muddle I would be called upon to untangle in the middle of the night. I spent the evening removing my mind from all thoughts of murder by reading Robert Hooke's[174] *Micrographia*.[175] Murder does not flourish among statements so charming as this: "The Louse is a Creature so officious, that 'twill be known to everyone at one time or other, so busie, and so impudent, that it will be intruding itself in every one's company, and

171 Robert Theodore Gunther (1869-1940) was a historian of science and founder of the Museum of History of Science in Oxford.

172 The first volume of *Early Science in Oxford* appeared in 1923, and the fourteenth in 1945. A fifteenth volume, by his son in 1950, dealt with Robert Gunthert himself.

173 This is a reflection on Todd himself and his bibliomania; he refers to his shelves in Mecklenburgh as book-hammocks.

174 Robert Hooke (1635-1703) was one of the outstatnding scientists of his day and was a member of the Royal Society's Council, as well as being its 'curator of experiments'.

175 *Micrographia: Or, Some Physiological Descriptions of Minute Bodies Made by Magnifying Glasses* was published by the Royal Society in 1665 and provided details of Hooke's observations with various types of lens.

so proud and aspiring withall, that it fears not to trample on the best, and affects nothing so much as a Crown; feeds and lives very high, and that makes it so saucy, as to pull any one by the ears that comes in its way, and will never be quiet till it has drawn blood."

It occurred to me that the louse, as described by Hooke, had a good deal in common with a number of people whom I knew. With this as a night-cap I went to bed, feeling that the Professor could fend for himself when he returned. There was no reason for me to play the anxious parent sitting up for the return of the erring offspring. I did not sleep deeply.

Round about one o'clock I heard a noise in the house. My first thoughts were that it might be burglars, but then I realised that even the very rashest burglars never went about their business making noises like a herd of rogue elephants out on the loose.

For a few minutes I lay still, enjoying the warmth which I had so sedulously engendered in my bed. The noise, if possible, grew greater and greater. Hell, I said to myself, the old man is tearing the house down, looking for something. I knew that I would pay for the carnage in the morning, for I would need to try and restore order to the chaos. Rather grumpily I heaved myself from my comfort and pulled an old battle-dress on over my pyjamas.

The Professor was in the middle of his room. All the cupboards were open and most of their contents were scattered round the room. When I considered my evening's reading it was completely fitting that he should be holding a microscope in his hand.

"'Ullo," he turned to greet me, "I'd the hell o' a time findin' this instrument."

"Did you think of looking in the cupboard where it should be kept?" I enquired rather coldly.

"Um," he sounded a little shy, "as a matter o' fact I didn't think o' that till I'd tried all the other cupboards. Ye see I'd had it out the other day an' I didn't remember puttin' it away again. Ye know how things are?"

"I put it away," I said, "and as I put it away it was probably in its proper place. Why didn't you come and ask me where it was before you started wrecking the house?"

"I didn't want to wake you," he replied and apologised handsomely. I started tidying up and, as I worked my anger evaporated. There was no future in being angry with the Professor; one might as well try pouring water over a cormorant in the hope of wetting it. I finally got things straight and turned to see what Professor Stubbs was up to. He had the microscope on his table, having cleared a space for it by sweeping the accumulation of papers and books to one side.

Beside the microscope was one of the round, screw-top jars which are used to contain meat-pastes, face-creams and so on. From this the Professor was removing a little sticky substance. He placed it on a slide.

I wandered over to take a look at it. The old man had his eyes to the microscope and was adjusting it. He screwed up his face as he turned to me.

"Look 'ee, Max," he mumbled, "ye'd better take a look. Ye saw me takin' the stuff out o' that jar. I'd like to know what ye think o' it."

I peered through the microscope. What I saw seemed familiar, but I suppose I was still half asleep. I just couldn't place them for the life of me. They were certainly familiar. I felt that the identification was just on the tip of my tongue, but I couldn't find the name for it.

Professor Stubbs produced a small box of slides. His air as he did this was that of the conjuror who removes the hundredth pigeon from his top-hat.

He slipped one of the slides into the microscope and beckoned to me to have another look.

What I saw was very nearly the same as those on the slide he had just prepared. There were, however, slight differences.

"What the hell are they?" I asked peevishly. It was all very well to be hauled from my bed in the middle of the night, but to have riddles propounded to me at that hour seemed to be going just a little bit too far.

"Can't ye guess?" he asked. There was something about his attitude that I didn't like. He seemed to be less cheerful than usual.

"No, I can't guess," I replied, "my brain doesn't work so well on just getting out of bed. What are they?"

He sighed heavily and then blew through his lips. He ran his hand through his mop of grey hair.

"They're spores o' fungi," he announced, "look through the box an' see if ye can find one that seems identical. It should be there, if I'm right."

I started taking slides from the box and popping them in and out of the microscope. I tried about half a dozen of these slides before I found one that appeared to be absolutely the same. I looked at the slide the old man had made once more and then again at that I had selected. There was no doubt about it. They were identical.

I removed the slide from the microscope and looked at the little label on it. It read *Amanita phalloides.*

"Where the hell did you get your specimen?" I demanded.

He was horribly evasive. "Maybe I brewed it up meself," he said, "an' then again, maybe I didn't. See here," he kicked a basket that was lying on the floor, "look at these."

I bent down and looked at the basket. It was filled with Death Caps. I was by this time feeling pretty fed up with the very sound of the things and I remembered that I had collected some for the Professor when I had been down in the country.

"What do you want all these for?" I asked, "I brought you quite a lot the other day and surely you didn't want any more?"

"Oh," he waved his hand airily, "it's just that I want to try a little experiment wi' 'em an' I had to have 'em fresh. As for where I got me specimen in that jar – well, ye'd better just let that ride till I know whether I'm wrong or whether I'm right. What ha' ye bin doin' wi' yerself all day?"

He stumped over to the barrel of beer and drew off some of it. It never seems to matter what time of the day or night it is. The Professor is always ready for a drink. I did not really want a pint myself, but I realised that I was in for an inquisition, so I accepted it and sat down in front of the fire, which I doctored with logs until it started to crackle cheerfully.

Professor Stubbs sat down and went through the rigmarole of preparing his pipe for action. He was obviously waiting.

"Well," I began, "I thought I might as well do a bit of detecting on my own, so I went down to Mecklenburgh Square and got hold of Roger. I discovered that he suspects Alec Dolittle of having murdered Stella."

The old man wagged his head wisely and his hair flopped up and down.

"So he thinks that, do he?" he said, more or less to himself, "an' why, Max, does he pick on Dolittle rather than on any of the others?"

"He gave me very good reasons why none of the others could have done it," I said and the Professor looked mildly surprised. "The only thing," I felt mildly ashamed of myself, but I had to still that doubt, "that occurred to me was the wonder whether, by any chance, he could have done the killings himself. That," I was explosive, "is why I loathe murders. They start me suspecting everyone, and I must say that I think it is beastly when I begin wondering whether or not one of my friends is the culprit. I wish that I had not had that thought, but since I've had it I feel I should ask you about it. What do you think?"

The Professor shook his head heavily. He did not seem to be at all happy. I could not understand what was the matter with him. He was usually cock-a-hoop when he had made a discovery and I was convinced that he had made some discovery during the day. He took a long pull at his beer and then relit his pipe with his ferocious petrol lighter. Once his head was comfortably swathed in vile smoke he looked at me through it.

"I'm not thinkin', Max," he said, "at the moment I'm collectin' facts an' I don't like them at all." He suddenly reverted to the subject of my day. "What makes Roger Sharon think that none o' the household, wi' the exception o' Alec Dolittle could ha' bin the murderer?"

One of my blessings is a fairly accurate memory, so I set to work to tell him exactly what Roger had said about Douglas, Harold and Alec Dolittle. Professor Stubbs took a butt-end of pencil and an old envelope from his pocket and made notes as I was speaking.

When I had finished I waited for his comments. He made none. He just looked into the fire and said nothing. I realised that he was a tired man. There were unusual creases round the corners of his eyes. I made an effort to get a reply from him. I thought that the sooner I could get him to go to bed the better.

"Well," I asked, "what do you think of that? Do you agree with what Roger said about these people, or do you think that he is trying to clear those whom he likes at the expense of Dolittle thrown to the lions?"

"It might be that, Max boy," he said heavily, "but there's a lot o' suggestive stuff in what ye just bin tellin' me. I'll need to think it over. Ye remember that Dolittle was down in the country at the time when everyone was gatherin' the mushrooms an' the *Amanita*, eh? Well, ye see, I can't make up me mind if that's helpful or if it's a hindrance to me. I can't make up me mind what his part is in the case. As for yer suspicion that Roger might ha' murdered Stella, well, I'll say that for ye, that it was an intelligent thought an' that ye might ha' gone more wrong than ye did."

"What do you mean?" I asked. "Do you mean that you think that Roger did murder Stella and then killed Loftus to try and cover his tracks? Do you mean that?"

"I'm not sayin' what I mean," he replied, "I'm still in a kinda muddle meself. I don't like it at all. Ye see I feel morally certain that I know who did the murder an' why it was done, but I daren't say anythin' yet."

"Why?" I demanded, "You know that I'm not in the habit of shooting off my mouth to everyone I know about your business."

He looked at me and smiled. It was a nice smile and as kindly as he could make it.

"No, no, Max," he protested, "I'm not suggestin' that ye'd go broadcasting yer suspicions around the place. But ye must realise that these people know ye, an' that if I was to tell ye that I suspected one o' 'em, there might be just that shade o' difference in yer attitude which 'ud give it away. I can't risk that at the moment. I am afraid o' what I bin findin' out an' I don't like it at all. I don't want to start sprayin' me beliefs around until I'm a bit more certain than I am at the present time. Ye mustn't think, Max, that because I'm not tellin' you now that I'm playin' mysterious, for I'm not. I like playin' mysterious as much as any of the detectives in the story books – it gives me a kick – but here I'm just not riskin' tellin' you what I found, as I don't want to make any unnecessary trouble. Ye understand, do ye?"

I have lived with the Professor long enough to know that there is no point in arguing with him when he has made up his mind. One might just as well try and move an army mule – but then there are people who try to move mules and sometimes they are successful. I am not one of nature's mule movers. Anyhow, I gathered that he was not trying to be obstinate this evening. He was just unsure of himself and he would not risk his ideas out in the open till they were properly set in his mind.

He was looking round the room and his eyes fell on the blue bound volumes of *Early Science in Oxford*.

"Oy, Max," he grunted, "you bein' extravagant, eh?" He hauled himself out of the chair and wandered over to them. "Ye are an expensive minded puppy," he grumbled, "here ye are buyin' facsimiles[176] o' books which we ha' the originals o' in the house. Why didn't ye just buy the volumes that ye wanted?"

"I can't stand broken sets," I said defensively, "and anyhow, I thought it would be a good idea to have the whole thing for reference."

He looked at my marker in the Louse in *Micrographia*. Then he turned over the pages of the book until he came to the engraving of sections of cork. This set him off. His tiredness dropped from him like a towel from a man who has dried himself. He wandered over to the shelves and took

176 The series employed the Replika process to produce facsimiles of selected scientific works, though without preserving their original size.

down the original edition of the book. I had to admit that it was far nicer than my Replika process facsimile.[177] I began to feel frightened. Once the old man gets going there's no knowing when he'll get to bed.

However, he took the book over to his table and his eye lighted on the microscope. He sat down at it and solemnly went through the process of trying every single slide in the box and comparing each with the slide he had prepared from the sticky smears inside the screw-top jar.

"I can't be wrong," he grumbled to himself, "it's just impossible that there should be anything else which I could mistake for it. Um. Um."

He shook his head slowly and made some notes on a piece of paper. Then he looked over at me. I was dozing quietly, watching the leaping log-flames through half-closed eyes.

"Max," he boomed, "I'd like ye to come over here an' prepare another slide from the stuff in this pot."

"Why on earth do you want that?" I was astonished. "Surely the slide you prepared yourself is good enough. It seemed all right to me."

"We might as well be sure," he replied, "after all, I bin handlin' *Amanita* meself an' I might just ha' put some spores on the slide. I'd like ye to pre-pare another one, so that there can be no suspicion that the slides are wrong. 'Ull ye do that afore ye go to yer bed?"

I hoisted myself out of the chair and went across to the table. I set to work carefully with clean slides which I took from the cupboard and I worked with clean instruments. I took my specimen from part of the jar which the Professor had not disturbed.

When I had finished I cleared the stuff away and then slipped the slide into the microscope. There was no doubt about it. The spores were those of *Amanita phalloides*, or at least they were more like that than they resembled any of the others of which we had specimens.

The Professor carefully sealed the sides of the slide with sticky paper and then he wrote his name across so that the writing would show if any-one fiddled with it. He then asked me to do the same. I did it. I must admit that I thought that it was a lot of fuss about nothing. It seemed to me that there was no doubt about the identity of the spores and that no power on earth could change them into anything else. I said as much.

He looked at me seriously. "Ye know, Max," he said sententiously, "I'll

177 The Replika process was a trademarked technique for lithographic printing owned by Peter Lund, Humphries Ltd. of Bradford.

admit that ye're tired an' that ye're half-asleep, but ye do seem to me to be a bit obtuse. Ye know the way that the Bishop's always gettin' at me for me failure to produce evidence for me deductions. Well, now I got a bit o' evidence, an' I want to be able to wave it under his nose an' crow, an' I'm not going to let him get away wi' sayin' that I made it meself."

The thought of what he was going to say to the Chief Inspector had cheered him to some extent, but he still looked slightly depressed.

"What's the matter," I asked, "are you not feeling well?"

"Oh," he looked startled by my question, "I'm feelin' all right in me body. It's just that me mind keeps on millin' away an' it can see no pleasant solution to the problem. Now, Max, I'm thinking it was time ye went back to yer bed. I got plenty I want ye to do in the mornin'." He pulled out his immense watch and glared at it. He seemed surprised that it pointed to a quarter to three. "By God," he was explosive, "it's quite time ye were sleepin', for I'll need ye bright an' early."

Even if I had felt like it, I did not think that there was any point in arguing. I suggested that he also should go to bed and he nodded his head wisely.

"I'll go when I've finished," he rumbled, "now ye'd better make the best o' the short time ye got left to ye. Good night."

Up the stairs I went again. I was worried by the Professor's appearance but I did not see that I could do anything about it. He would go to bed when he was ready and not a minute before. Once or twice he had pointed out to me that as a man grew older he needed less sleep. I did not altogether believe this theory, as I remembered how, when I'd been very young, I'd think nothing of sitting up all night, speaking about things that seemed to affect the future of the world, and how I'd then go out and do a day's work. Nowadays, I find, I need between six and eight hours.

I had no sooner laid my head on the pillow – thanking God that the poltergeist had not filled my bed with books while I was out of it – than I was fast asleep.

CHAPTER SEVENTEEN

ALL LIT UP LIKE A CHRISTMAS TREE

I was still sleepy when I woke to the unearthly horror of my alarm clock. I keep it out of range of my arm as otherwise I am inclined to reach over to turn it off, and then go back to sleep. The damned thing buzzed away unmercifully. I hauled myself from between the sheets and staggered across the room to extinguish it.

Once I was out of bed there was no point in crawling back again to sleep for a dubious half-hour, tormented by the thought that I should be up and dressed. I hauled myself off to the bathroom and did the necessary things in the way of bathing and shaving.

When I got down the Professor was still sitting at his table. I did not believe that he had been to bed at all, although he had certainly managed to shave at some period of the night. The face he turned towards me was certainly gloomy, but the tiredness had vanished from the corners of his eyes.

"Good morning," I said politely. "Did you manage to sleep all right?"

He grunted in a noncommittal kind of way. I could see then that my guess had been right and that he had not been to bed at all. I turned round and walked to the door of his room. The bed was undisturbed. I wheeled and went back to him.

"Look here," I said sternly, "if you won't sleep you can't expect to keep going. You go to bed now and spend the day resting and I'll do all that you want me to do, exactly as you want it done. I can do nearly everything that has to be done without worrying you in the least. For God's sake go and get a rest. Apart from all other considerations, I don't want you to become ill. Think of the extra work it would throw on my shoulders and see if you don't think it selfish of you to work yourself to a frazzle."

I thought I was being terribly cunning by adopting a purely selfish attitude to his behaviour. It was the one way I might have made him obey my suggestion. I might have irritated him into going to bed. He raised a sombre face towards me and creased it with an unreal smile.

"That's no go, Max," he said deeply, "you won't get me to bed that way. I got to go on at the moment. I'll rest when I got everythin' straight in me mind. Till then, tho', I got to keep goin'. I got a lot to do today an' I got work for ye to do, too."

The smile he gave me was meant, but the effect was that of a sad and distressed man trying to face the world bravely. I felt on top of the world.

We had breakfast without the usual bickering. I was seriously worried about the Professor. Even when he had had to go and try and arrest the maiden niece of the murdered bookseller[178] he had not looked so gloomy. There must be something besides the murder on his mind, I told myself, there must be.

After breakfast we retired to his room. I felt as though I was one of Napoleon's *aides-de-camps* receiving his orders before the battle of Waterloo. I didn't know whose Waterloo it was to be, but judging from the look on his face I guessed that the Professor was afraid that it would be his.

He sat slumped in the chair in front of his table, looking at the notes he had made on the backs of envelopes and the blank pages of letters. He scowled at these notes ferociously. He read right through them once more and then he tore the whole packet into fragments, destroying the Lord alone knows how many important and unanswered letters in the process. Even that failed to draw a reproof from me. I was lying low and waiting.

He swung the heavy chair round to face me. I made some show of being busy with the papers on my table. It did not deceive him. His face showed clearly that he had made up his mind about what he meant to do.

"I'm givin' a dinner party tonight, Max," he said unexpectedly, "an' I want ye to go into the highways an' byways an' collect me guests. I want all the people who are concerned in these thunderin' deaths to be present here tonight an' I want ye to go an' invite them. That means there'll be yer Mary, Roger Sharon, Harold Ironside, Alec Dolittle, an' Douglas Newsome, as well as ourselves. It's a monstrous deal o' male to very little woman, but that can't be helped. I want ye to go an' get them yerself. That means I want ye to deliver me message personally."

"Roger's on the phone," I said helpfully, "it would be much easier to ring

---

178 See *Bodies in a Bookshop*, published by John Westhouse in 1946 and reprinted by Dover in 1984.

them up and ask them along."

For the first time there was some return of the Professor Stubbs I was accustomed to dealing with. He growled at me fiercely.

"Ye'd better do as ye're told, Max," he said, "I got me reasons. Now, what I got to say is most important. I want ye to note if anyone tries to excuse themselves or says they can't come. Ye've got to get 'em here, even if it means tellin' all the lies ye can think o'. Ye can blame it all on me. Let's see now." He creased his forehead to give the impression that he was thinking deeply. I was not impressed, for it was obvious to me that he'd been working these things out during the hours when I had been sleeping. "Let's see now, in the case o' yer girl, she's the only one who's really workin' – she might be called back to her work. Well, I'll ring her theatre for her, so if she says she can't come, ye can tell her I've fixed it. An' as for the others, if they got previous appointments, they'll just dam' well have to postpone them. I got to have 'em all here, so's I can say what I got to say an' say it direct, wi'out any hearsay about it."

He paused and ran his hand through his hair. It was the hand that was holding his pipe, and fragments of tobacco and ash were left mingled with the grey hair. With the sorrowful look on his face and the ashes in his hair, all that he needed was the sackcloth and he'd have been a full-blown penitent.

"I'll tell ye what, Max," he went on, "it wouldn't do any harm if ye were to do a bit o' spreadin' o' alarm and despondency. Ye can kinda suggest wi'out bein' too definite that I got a thunderin' good idea o' the identity o' the killer. Ye'll find that bit kinda easy for I see ye're thinkin' that maybe I ha' an idea. Well, o' course, I ha', but I'm not yet in a position where I can start broadcastin' it. I'd like ye to stress that I'm being secretive, even to yerself – if it's not too damagin' to yer pride – for that'll help me a lot. Can ye do it?"

I nodded my head. There was no doubt that if the old man wanted me to start rumours I was in a position to do so. He had not told me a thing from which I could make sense, and there's nothing like knowing nothing if one wants to start rumours flying around. A rumour has to have a bit of truth to it to make it sound real, but there need be no more truth in one than there is effective drug in a patent medicine.

I went and put on a tie and prepared to depart. I looked into the room as I passed. The Professor was still sunk in his desk. He seemed to be trying whether he could not twiddle his thumbs in opposite directions. If he'd had a bit of string he'd have been playing cat's cradles.[179] He was as aimless as a rook drifting in the wind. I shut the door quietly and went out.

Roger agreed to come to dinner in the evening and he went round the house with me asking the others.

Douglas Newsome was as willing as Roger and so was Harold. The only trouble came from Alec Dolittle. He grumbled at being hauled out to Hampstead. He said that he had promised to have a drink with an old friend in *The Bodega*[180] in Chancery Lane.[181] It was not helpful. I suggested he pushed around there during the lunch session and left a message for his friend. I told Mary that the Professor was ringing up Linton and making arrangements for her to be excused for the evening.

She looked relieved. "That's all right then, darling," she said, "I really should have gone back this afternoon, but I'll stay over till tomorrow."

I suggested that she should lunch with me, but I gathered that she had already promised to lunch with Douglas, Harold and Roger. Alec Dolittle, I noticed, had dropped out of the party. Rather tentatively, I suggested that I might join them for lunch.

We all drifted round to *The Lamb* when it opened and I took the opportunity of doing my alarm and despondency stuff, because if Alec was not with us I would have no chance to do it during lunch.

I must say that they took it very well indeed. They hardly looked at one another though my statement was a direct invitation to each to become suspicious of the one next to him. Alec Dolittle was the only one whom the news seemed to affect. He spilt some of his beer and then gulped the remainder.

"I say," he exclaimed, looking up at the clock, "I've just remembered I promised to meet someone in *The Cock*[182] ten minutes ago. I'll need to dash. Thanks for the drink. See you this evening, Boyle."

I realised that Roger was watching me and I nodded my head meaningly. I was now quite convinced that Alec Dolittle was the murderer. I was rather

179 A game in which string is looped over the fingers to creat intricate patterns and designs.

180 *The Bodega* was in operation in 1896 and was previously known as *The Hole in the Wall*.

181 New Lane, built in the time of Henry III, eventually became known as Chancellor's Lane, and finally Chancery Lane. It passes by the Inns of Court which lie at the heart of the legal profession in London.

182 Probably *The Cock Tavern* in Great Portland Street.

surprised at the Professor's rashness in asking me to spread his knowledge around so early in the morning. It meant that Dolittle had a whole day's start on the police and that he might even manage to get away abroad.

As I thought of this I wondered vaguely if the old man had found some sort of extenuating circumstance about the murders, which had prompted him to give Dolittle the chance of escaping. I could see that there might have been an extenuating point in killing Arthur Loftus, but I could see none in connection with the death of Stella.

Roger bought a round of drinks. The conversation became general. It seemed that the subject of murder was to be avoided by everyone. I could not say that I was sorry that there seemed to be a mutually established taboo on the subject. As the R.A.F. used to say when they had failed to have anything: I'd had it.[183]

All the same, I kept turning over the subject of Stella Mortimer in my mind. I remembered that Arthur Loftus had said that she was an all the way round bitch. Of course, he had been as spiteful as a skunk in a temper, but still there might have been something in it. Perhaps she had bitched Alec Dolittle so thoroughly that he had murdered her. He seemed, thinking it over, the sort of man who might use poison. He was a physical weakling and poison sometimes acts as the strong arm for those who have not the power to kill by violence. I found myself making excuses for him. It might be that he had not known the awfulness of death by fungus poisoning. After all, until I had stumbled into this case I was under the impression, myself, that the effects were narcotic and not violent. That one more or less swept one's life away. I did not know of the continuous diarrhoea and vomiting.

I suddenly realised that Mary was speaking to me. I felt pretty ashamed of myself. It was ridiculous that I should get my mind so tied up in a murder that I should be unable to concentrate upon what the girl I adored was saying to me. The only relief was that there was nothing of importance in her words. She was only suggesting that we should eat at *Bertorelli's*[184] in Charlotte Street[185] and go along before the crowds got there so as to get a decent table.

183 i.e. you won't get it, you're too late.

184 The first Bertorelli's restaurant was established in 1913 by the Bertorelli brothers primarily to provide food to taxi drivers and chauffeurs.

185 Charlotte Street was built in 1763 and named after Queen Charlotte, the wife of King George III.

The lunch was fairly cheerful. Nobody seemed to be casting their ideas forward to the evening. They seemed to be content with what they had at the moment.

It seemed to me that I managed to get rather more than my fair share of Mary's conversation and this was all to the good as far as I was concerned.

Even Douglas Newsome seemed to be in better fettle than was commonly the case. He told one or two funny stories, which were against himself, and he actually refused to take a drink when I realised that he had emptied his glass before the rest of us.

The best parties have to break up some time and we parted when *The Fitzroy* closed. Everyone seemed to be prepared for the evening, so I wandered along to the Tottenham Court Road[186] and caught a 24 bus. Once I was on it I fell to thinking about the way people had taken my various announcements.

I had to make some sort of report to the old man when I got home, so I thought I'd better get my ideas in order. The trouble was that, with the exception of Alec Dolittle, everyone had taken the invitation and my rumour-mongering as a matter of course. They had all seemed only too pleased to come.

Professor Stubbs was digging in the garden when I arrived. It is very seldom indeed that I see him taking any exercise so I was astonished, particularly as I'd thought him too weary to stir from his chair.

"Hullo," I said cheerfully, "are you trying to get your weight down? Why don't you have a Turkish bath? It's much less tiring."

He grunted and drove the fork hard into the ground. "How'd yet get on?" he demanded, "Are they all comin'?"

I told him exactly what had happened. I pointed out that, although I knew it was none of my business, I thought it was rash to tell Alec Dolittle in the morning that he was proposing to unmask him as a murderer in the evening.

He just nodded his head solemnly. I suggested that perhaps it would be a good idea to get hold of the Bishop and get him to set his men in pursuit of Dolittle. I offered to go and telephone as he had such difficulty with the

---

186 Tottenham Court Road is named after William de Tottenhall who owned a manor house in the area in the 13th century. It heads north from Oxford Street, as a continuation of Charing Cross Road, and meets Euston Road at about its middle.

machine. He stopped me, waving a large and mud-hung hand.

"No, no, Max," his voice was mild, "you just let things be. I know what I'm doin'. I tell ye that Alec Dolittle'll be there to dinner even if none o' the others turn up. You leave the matter o' the police to me. I can deal wi' 'em in me own time an' in me own way. Now I got somethin' else I want ye to do for me. I want ye to go an' buy me a couple o' pounds o' mushrooms. I want to serve 'em up for dinner."

I looked at him in frank astonishment.

"Are you sure you don't think a rest would do you good?" I asked, really anxiously, "I have never heard of anything so tactless in my life. Here you go, inviting people to dinner who have just suffered the death of a friend by fungus poisoning, and you have the appalling nerve and lack of taste to offer them mushrooms."

"You just do as you're told," he mumbled, "I know what I'm doin'. I want ye to get me field mushrooms, an' not the cultivated ones if ye can manage it. I don't mind what they cost, but get field ones if ye can. If ye can't, choose a basket o' rather fully grown cultivated ones, the raggeder the better, an' they may pass as field mushrooms. If yer friends don't feel like eatin' mushrooms, you an' I can eat 'em. After all, Max, I like mushrooms."

The tone in which he uttered this last remark was piteous and I did not feel that it was my job to argue with him if he really had made up his mind to be completely tactless. I had the hell of a hunt for field mushrooms and finally got right back to town in my search for them. I ran them to earth finally in a shop in St Martin's Lane. By this time I was getting irritable, so I took a taxi all the way home with them and over-tipped the driver.

I announced my extravagance to the Professor, but all he did was to pull a crumpled pound note from his pocket and pass it to me.

"Maybe this'll pay for the mushrooms an' the taxi," he said, "I'm sorry that I had to send you on such a chase, but then ye see I need the mushrooms very badly."

He was seated at his table and spread over the paper and so on was *The Times*. As he turned back he knocked this off and I saw what had been hidden under the paper. There lay the basket which had held the *Amanita phalloides* and beside it, neatly stacked in a bowl, were the damned things themselves.

Professor Stubbs had been engaged in peeling them. A pile of shavings of greenish grey lay beside him.

"Good God," I said blankly, "what the hell's this? Supper for the Borgias? Look here, sir," I was really serious, "you can't go feeding these things to people and hope to get away with it. They're deadly poison. You'll bump someone off if you're not careful. I read that article in the *B.M.J.* and though it does say something about anti-phalloidien serum having excellent results if given within a reasonable time of the onset of symptoms, I still wouldn't care to risk the stuff. It's one hell of a death."

The old man peeled another Death Cap slowly and carefully. He placed it with the rest of his pile.

"Ye needn't worry, Max," he said gloomily, "no one's goin' to eat them. I'm just tryin' an experiment to please meself. I want to see what they look like cooked. There's no chance o' them getting mixed wi' Mrs. Farley's cookin'. Ye needn't be frightened o' eatin' anythin' ye may see served at the table this evenin', an' ye needn't worry at anythin' I do or say. I got me reasons an' all I ask is that ye'll gi' me a hand in carryin' out me intentions."

He rose to his feet and picked up the bowl and the piece of skin and discarded specimens of the fungi themselves. He dumped the skins and the fungi in the fire and waited until they had frizzled away.

"Ye'd better make that fire in the mornin'," he observed to me in a sepulchral tone, "there's a poison in these things which ain't destroyed by heat, and we don't want to find it turnin' up at breakfast. Ye ha' the sense to wash yer hands properly an' ye ha' the time to do it. I'm not saying that Mrs. Farley wouldn't do as much, but I'd rather ye did it."

I was flattered. There was no other word for it. Used as I am to the old man's craziness and perversity, this really seemed to be the top of his Himalayas.

He stumped out of the room and through the hall. In the garden he made for the hut where he sometimes does experiments. It's a place furnished with a bench and stools and it has gas and electricity laid on. I could see that the old man had been there before, preparing his materials. There was a frying pan standing beside a gas-ring which had temporarily supplanted the bunsen.

If I'd had any astonishment left in me it would have been forced out when the Professor set to work solemnly to cook the beastly things. I could only be inane. "Don't go tasting the fungi in the approved cook manner," I said, "they have an unpleasant effect on your inside."

He looked round from his ploy. The *Amanita phalloides* were bubbling away nicely in milk. He decanted the result into a small dish. I had to admit that I could not have told them from ordinary mushrooms. The only difference was that there was no smell, none of the familiar flavour of cooked mushrooms. Otherwise the dish would have deceived me even if I'd been suspicious. He asked me for my opinion. I gave it to him, carefully refraining from embroidering my idea that the cuckoos had finally got him.

"Um," he said unhappily, bending over the witches' brew and sniffing heartily. "Um, maybe, ye're right. But," his face lightened momentarily, "but ye could correct that in a moment if ye'd plenty o' mushrooms around. Ye'd just decant some o' the gravy or broth or whatever ye call it over them an' no one 'ud be able to tell the difference. D'ye think they would?"

I assured him gravely that I was quite sure that his hell's stew would deceive anyone if only he was taught to smell the right way. I could not say with equal truth that I was looking forward to eating mushrooms for supper, even if I knew they were all right. I accompanied the Professor back to the house and left him, still planning things, while I went up and had a bath. If I was to be poisoned by the old crackpot, I told myself, at least I'd take it clean, and make certain that none of the blasted spores could have drifted on to me.

CHAPTER EIGHTEEN

DINNER FOR DEATH

THE OLD man was right. Alec Dolittle was the first to arrive. He was not noticeably sober, but neither was he shockingly drunk. I felt that I was having at least a couple of Ossas piled on my Pelion.[187] The old man had the nerve to push off about some game of his own and leave me to entertain Dolittle.

I had never before tried to play social host to a man whom I was convinced was a murderer. It wouldn't have been so bad if I could have shown him my feelings, but I'd gathered from the Professor that I was to play host as though there was nothing wrong. I gave him a glass of sherry and took one myself. We exchanged a few trivialities and after that the conversation stuck. Dolittle got up and walked round the room, looking at the books in the shelves. He showed a surprising knowledge of the books and I expressed my astonishment.

"Oh," he said, "once when I was stuck in Germany I got a job doing a catalogue of this kind of book. It was a large library which had been collected by a balmy count and his heirs were thinking of selling it, but they felt that they might as well know what they had before they parted with it. They didn't pay well, but at that time it was better than a smack in the belly with a wet fish, and I picked up quite a lot of odd information and a copy of the *Almanach de Gotha*[188] out of it."

He bent down to look at the folios in their calf and red labels. I realised exactly what Roger had meant when he said that Alec Dolittle talked the

---

187 In Greek mythology Mount Pelion was piled on Mount Ossa by the giants Otus and Ephialtes (not Ossa on Pelion).

188 The *Almanach de Gotha* is a directory of royal and noble families which was first published by C.W. Ettinger in 1763. It came to an end in 1944 when the Soviets destroyed the archives of the then publisher, Justus Perthes, but was revived in 1998 by Boydell & Brewer.

hell of a lot but without giving away information about himself. Thinking over what he had said, all I could deduce from his remarks was that he'd travelled a lot and had been broke. No dates and no personal details. And I already knew that he'd been round the world and was usually penniless.

I thought of several ways of re-opening the conversation but when I examined them the words I was going to use seemed too trivial and, anyhow, I decided, there was not much use in talking. I was saved further embarrassment by the appearance of the rest of the party and the old man himself. He did the honours with drinks as if he was dealing out the elixir of life at a penny hot spring. I have noticed that he sometimes seems to be playing a part to himself. Tonight I felt that he was doing the part of a barker outside a fair-stall; a show which was on the point of bankruptcy, but which might have been saved if he called "Walk up, walk up!" loud enough.

I managed to get next to Mary. She was looking very beautiful and rather excited. The flush on her cheeks suited her. I felt that she was indeed a wonderful girl, and I hoped that somehow I'd persuade her to fall for me as hard as I had fallen for her.

"Hullo, Max darling," she greeted me, and as usual I tried to read more than the usual theatrical affection into the word. She squeezed my arm, "Isn't this exciting?"

I would hardly have been so pleased about it myself, but then I'd been mixed up in murder cases before and I must say that I don't like the final act of any of them, even when it seems to me that the murderer deserves to be boiled alive in hydrochloric acid. All the same, if Mary was really interested in me, there was no reason for her to care what happened to the others and, in addition, I supposed that, like Roger, she had decided for herself that Alec Dolittle was the guilty person.

I realised that the Professor had bumbled across to Alec and was talking to him about the books. I noticed he pulled one or two out to show them off and put them back in the wrong places. I sighed. Mary heard my sigh.

"What's the matter, darling?" she asked and I pointed indignantly with my thumb.

"It's him," I said inelegantly, "he will take books and put them back in the wrong places and then he complains when he can't find them. It falls back on me to restore order."

The Professor heard my words and turned guiltily. He was meant to hear them. Mary laughed. "You shouldn't mind him, Professor Stubbs," she said cheerfully, "he's an awful old cross-patch sometimes, aren't you, darling?"

Although I felt that I was completely in the right I let her affection overrule my feelings of indignation and joined in the general conversation.

Roger, I noticed, had picked up a copy of Nehemiah Grew's[189] *Anatomy of Plants*,[190] 1682, and was engaged in studying the beautiful plates of cross-sections of different plants, seen through a microscope.

"Why the devil, Max," he said, looking at me, "did you never tell me about these? They are fantastically wonderful. I wonder where I could get a copy of this book?"

The old man turned. "I think we got an incomplete copy," he boomed, "it ain't got all the plates, and it ain't got much o' the text, but ye're welcome to that if ye'd like it. Where the devil has that copy got to, Max?"

"You see, Mary," I said, taking a belated triumph, "he needs to ask me where everything is. He hasn't got the slightest idea himself where to find a thing in this house."

There was something unreal about the whole gathering. To the casual eye it might have seemed to be nothing more than an ordinary social evening. The chit-chat was unconcerned with anything beyond the ordinary trivialities. But, behind the persiflage and the light-heartedness, I could feel that there was a cold wind blowing, a wind as cold as if it had swept over the Steppes of Russia, a wind which seemed to carry the howl of wolves pursuing their destined and helpless prey. I shivered as this idea came to me. I felt as though someone had walked over my grave.

I realised that Mary's hand was on my arm and she squeezed it. The contact with someone warm and live cheered me up.

Looking at my wrist watch I realised that there was another quarter of an hour to fill before it was time for supper. I looked round the room to see what signs of disturbance I could see in the rest of the party. There were none.

Douglas Newsome, I realised, was punishing the sherry pretty hard, but that could hardly be taken as a sign of a guilty conscience for he had

189 Nehemiah Grew (1641-1712) was an English botanist and one of the pioneers in the science of plant anatomy. His first paper on plant anatomy, *The Anatomy of Vegetables Begun*, was presented to the Royal Society in 1672.

190 *The Anatomy of Plants* was published in 1682 and was the first major text on plant structure based on microscopic observation and analysis. Todd was fortunate to own his own copy.

a habit of doing that to any drink that came near him. He was, I thought, mumbling to himself, but I guessed he was only reciting some snatch of verse that had occurred to him. If I had not seen him behaving in the same way when there was nothing wrong, I might have thought that he was worried about something. But as it was I knew it was only his psyche.

Harold and Roger were still looking at the Grew. I had found the tattered copy and passed it to them. Roger seemed immensely pleased by the present.

I could not understand the old man. He was looking as gloomy as a churchwarden or a professional mute at a funeral. He was talking to Alec Dolittle as though there was nothing wrong and as though he was not just about to announce that he had found the murderer. I went over and took the sherry from the vicinity of Douglas and circulated it. Then I put it back beside him. After all I wasn't paying for the stuff and I saw no reason why Douglas should not behave in character if he wanted to do so.

It seemed an interminable time before Mrs. Farley came and announced that dinner was ready. We filtered through into the dining-room. I saw that the old man had arranged the party round the table according to some scheme of his own.

He sat in his usual place. Douglas was on his right and Mary on his left. I sat between Mary and Harold. Then there was Roger and finally Alec Dolittle.

I don't know how the others felt when they sat down, but my own feelings were that I was sitting rather on the verge of an active volcano, one which might erupt fire and rubble at any moment. I can't say that I like the feeling, though I should be used to it by this time as one of the old man's habits is to make me feel like that.

"Harumph," the old man snorted, "I kinda think we'd better keep off the subject that's worryin' us all until we ha' had a bit o' somethin' to eat. What'll ye drink, Miss Winstone?"

The conversation became general. The Professor asked Roger about his painting, and, unusually, Roger was fairly communicative and told him quite a lot about it.

Sitting next to Mary I felt pretty cheerful, but I'd have felt better if we could have got the unpleasant business done before we ate. I might then have partaken of a hearty meal. As it was I rather pecked at things like a not too hungry sparrow.

Everything went perfectly smoothly until we arrived at the subject of a savoury.

Mrs. Farley brought in three dishes and placed them in front of the Professor. Two of these were a pair of Sheffield plate[191] dishes which were identical twins.

The Professor leaned forward and exposed the contents of them. They both seemed to contain mushrooms on toast.

He looked heavily round the table and cleared his throat gustily. He wiped his glasses with his ferocious looking bandana.

"Hum," he grunted, "now I got to get down to business. I bin experimentin' an' before ye ye'll see the results of me experiment. The dish on me right holds ordinary field mushrooms on toast an' that on me left *Amanita phalloides*. I just doctored the latter wi' a little mushroom juice an' I'd defy anyone to tell the difference, in either taste or smell. If I was to eat the dish on me left I'd die, but the other dish is quite harmless an' tasty." He glared round the table. "Now I tried this experiment as I wanted to prove to meself that anyone eatin' *phalloides* wouldn't know what they'd eaten till it was too late. Ye may think it tactless o' me to offer ye mushrooms – maybe it is, but there's the point that ye can't keep off 'em for the rest o' yer life, at least if ye got anythin' in the way o' palates an' I thought ye might as well start wi' them here, knowin' that they'd be safe. For, damme, I'm a blinkin' botanist an' I should know which are which."

I looked round the table. No one seemed to be able to think of a comment on this.

"However," the old man went on, "if any of ye think ye'd rather not eat o' mushrooms yet, ye can ha' angels-on-horseback.[192] I got Mrs. Farley to make some too ..."

At that moment the light in the room went out. The old man swore gustily. "Dam' that fuse," he said, "it's always doin' that at the wrong moment."

He rose to his feet and lumbered over to the door of the room. He threw it open and a faint trickle of light filtered through, not enough to let us see in the room, but enough to show where the door was.

191 Sheffield plate, a layered combination of silver and copper, was invented by Thomas Boulsover (1705-1788) in 1743 and allowed manufacturers to produce household items that looked identical to those made from solid silver but at a fraction of the cost.

192 A hot appetiser made from oysters wrapped in bacon.

"Max," the voice in the dark was heavy, "be a good chap an' go an' mend the fuse. I'd do it meself, but ye're quicker at it."

I got up and made for the door, wondering what sort of game the Professor was playing. I knew that he was up to something and that he had probably arranged the fuse himself, for I never remembered the lights going out like that before. When I got to the fuse-box I knew I had been right. Jim Farley was standing there, holding the little porcelain fuse in his hand. I was about to say something to him, but he put his finger to his lips and handed me the fuse. He turned and, on tiptoes, made for the door that led to his quarters. I spent a few seconds fiddling about, trying to occupy what I thought would be the right amount of time for me to mend the wire, then I shoved the piece of porcelain back into place.

"Is that all right now?" I shouted and I heard the Professor's bellow in the affirmative. I went back to the dining-room. Nothing seemed to have happened since I went out. I took my seat.

The Professor turned with a great show of old fashioned chivalry to Mary, "Will ye try me mushrooms?"

She shivered slightly. "I hope you won't mind, Professor," she said, "if I don't. I'd rather have the other thing. You see, Stella was my friend and it's still too recent."

I could have killed the old man. If my looks had been poisoned darts he'd have dropped in his chair. As it was he paid no attention to me. He went on round the table. There did not seem to be much demand for mushrooms. Douglas Newsome was the only person who accepted them.

There was something slightly theatrical about Douglas's behaviour, as if he was facing slightly fearful odds for some private reason of his own.

The old man dealt the angels-on-horseback. He did not offer me a choice, but passed me some mushrooms. For a moment I had a faint panic as I could not remember whether he had said that the *Amanita* were in the left hand or the right hand dish. I thought it would be just like the old man to make a mistake of that sort. I would go into the matter immediately after dinner, and if I found he had made a mistake I would be dosed with antiphalloidien serum.[193]

I remembered that the old man had said that I had nothing to fear, but

193 Dubash and Teare (see Chapter 14) state that the serum produced by Dujarric de la Rivière in 1933 "appears to have had excellent results when given within a reasonable time of onset of symptoms."

I wouldn't trust him. I tried the mushrooms. They did seem to have an awfully bitter taste. They didn't seem to taste like real mushrooms at all. I looked along the table and saw that the old man was gobbling his share up as if they were the most delicious things in the world. Douglas, too, seemed to be enjoying his plateful.

Probably it was a purely psychological reaction, I decided, and my fears of poison were making me lose my sense of taste. I ate up what was on my plate.

The old man seemed to have forgotten that he had been a very tactless old fool. He was talking quietly to Douglas. I listened in with half an ear and found that they were discussing Andrew Young's poems and his book *A Prospect of Flowers*.[194] I must say that I thought things were going a bit too far when he could switch his mind like that. It was all very well for him, but he had succeeded in making all his guests, except Douglas, thoroughly uncomfortable.

It did not seem that he was ready for his *dénouement* yet. He suggested that we should retire to the other room and have coffee there. Mrs. Farley had built up the log fire in our absence and it crackled and sparked in the large open fireplace.

Professor Stubbs did the honours with the coffee and offered everyone some brandy. I was glad to have it as I was feeling pretty groggy. I was quite sure that he had poisoned me with his damned *phalloides* on toast.

It might still have been an ordinary social evening. Everyone was sitting round the fire just like a normal party of people enjoying their coffee and brandy.

I started a whispered conversation with Mary. It seemed quite definite that she had to return to Linton the next day. This seemed to me to be pretty hard as I had made up my mind that I was getting along with her better than ever before and now my bubble was to be broken.

She held on to my arm tightly. "It's all right, Max darling," she said, "it won't be for long. I'll see you on Sunday and, then, I think I'm going to get a job in town so you can see me as often as you like – if you don't get tired of me first."

"Don't talk nonsense," I replied, "I won't grow tired of you. It's far more likely that you'll get fed up with me."

I felt as happy as the proverbial sandboy. I could have danced a mazurka

194 *A Prospect of Flowers* was published by Jonathan Cape in 1945.

across the floor. I wanted to kiss everyone in the room. I could have walked the tightrope.

The old man laid down his empty coffee cup. He clattered it into his saucer with an appalling noise. He grunted noisily. Everyone looked at him. He leaned forward towards me. I wondered what errand I was about to be given.

Then I realised that he was not looking at me, but at Mary. I didn't like the way he was looking at her.

"Um, Miss Winstone," he said slowly, "'Ud ye mind tellin' me why ye murdered Stella Mortimer?"

I felt Mary beside me becoming stiff and as rigid as a waxwork. I held on to her arm as tightly as I could. I glared at the Professor. It was all very well for him to have his joke if he wanted to have it, but I drew the line at this sort of thing. I started to rise from my seat.

"Sit down, Max!" the old man barked at me, angrily. I had never had that tone of voice employed on me before and I was so surprised by it that I sat down with the celerity of a bullock that has just been hit by a humane-killer. The trouble here was that the Professor had not used a humane-killer.

I looked at the others. Their faces displayed various shades of disbelief and astonishment, all except Douglas who had somehow manœuvred the brandy bottle into his keeping. He looked up at the rest of us in a vacant way. He spoke suddenly:

"Never to have lived is best, ancient writers say;
Never to have drawn the breath of life, never to have looked into the eye of day;
The second best's a gay good night and quickly turn away ..."[195]

"Shut up, Douglas," it was Roger. His tone of voice was as harsh as if his throat had been filled with chaff. "Shut up, you bloody little fool."

Douglas subsided, pouring more brandy into his glass. The Professor was still looking at Mary.

"No," he said deeply, "I'm not joking. I want ye to tell me why ye had to murder Stella. It's no use sayin' ye didn't do it, for I know ye did. I got me evidence."

He let his arm down beside his chair and fished up the little screw-top jar which contained the smears of *Amanita phalloides*. He held this

---

195 From *A Man Young and Old* by William Butler Yeats (1839-1922).

between a blunt finger and thumb.

Mary said nothing. She was clinging to my arm as if I was her one bulwark between life and the fires of hell. I put my hand over her arm.

"It's all right, Mary darling," I said as gently as I could, "you've only got to prove to him that you didn't do it and he'll go off an another wild goose chase. It's one of his hobbies. He tries to prove that any murder could have been committed by anyone who was anywhere near, and once he has done that and finds that he's wrong, he goes on and proves that someone else did the murder. He's bound to be right in the end, but it takes him the hell of a time to get there. Come on, show him that he is wrong."

She let go of my arm and rose slowly to her feet. She gave a sort of gasp. When she spoke her voice was as steady as the deck of a ship, but I could feel the throb beneath it.

"Oh, but you see, he's not wrong."

My world, the penny world I had built myself in dreams, fell round my shoulders like the last leaves from an oak in autumn. My dreams fluttered to the ground and were trodden underfoot. It was no consolation for me to tell myself that in that mould another acorn would germinate. Like Douglas a quotation came to me: "Cut is the branch that might haue growne ful straight, and burned is *Apolloes* Laurel bough."[196] The words brought me no comfort.

Time seemed to have stopped. I could hear the noisy tick of the old man's gargantuan watch, but there seemed to be an age between one tick and the next. I had become an actor in a slow motion film. My words dropped from my mouth as slowly as petals from an overblown rose.

"What do you mean, my darling," I squeezed the words out painfully, "what do you mean? You can't be serious, you can't. You wouldn't do a thing like that! You couldn't! You are too gentle, too kind!"

I did not realise that I was shouting. They only told me afterwards. Douglas came slowly across the room. It seemed that he was wearing diver's boots with immense lead weights on the soles. His movement was as slow as my mind. He tilted the bottle of brandy into my glass and held it out to me. I shook my head.

He persisted and I gave way. The brandy was like water. There would not have been a kick in a gallon of it.

196 From *Doctor Faustus* (Act 5, Scene 3) by Christopher Marlowe (1564-1593).

Mary was still standing up. She seemed to have relaxed and she was no longer shivering.

"Yes," she said steadily, "I killed Stella and I killed Arthur Loftus."

"But why?" I demanded, crying out against the senselessness of things.

She looked down at me. She might have been looking at a stone in a wall for all the feeling there was about that look. I was a dead thing in her mind, something which had once lived but which was now expended, the casing of a squib on a village green on the morning of November 6.

"All my life," she said slowly and carefully, "Stella has been ahead of me. She got the jobs that I should have had, and then she took away the man I wanted." She looked over at Roger. "You."

I have never seen a man look so startled as Roger looked then. He almost dropped his glass which was dangling aimlessly in his hand.

"Yes," Mary went on, "I could have forgiven her the jobs, for she was a good actress, even perhaps a better one than I am, but I could not forgive her that. I had to kill her."

The old man was trimming the end of a cigar carefully. He seemed to be quite uninterested in the proceedings.

"It was easy," Mary said, "she told me how to do it herself. She brought that little book in the King Penguin series down with her. She had bought it on the railway station. I read it up and I knew how to do it. I do not know a lot about plants and funguses, but I found I could tell the difference between mushrooms and these Death Cap things. I had seen them on the edge of a wood. So I went and collected some of them and boiled them up."

I remembered how she had avoided the little pan that day when she had given me coffee in her digs.

"I put some of the mess into a little jar and took it up to town, when I had made certain that we had gathered mushrooms from the field where the poison toadstools grew. Of course I could not leave the jar about Mecklenburgh Square, so I took it back to Linton with me and threw it away there."

Her voice seemed to have shed all feeling and all emotion, as a snake sheds its useless skin.

"I wanted Stella to suffer as she died, and she did suffer. I was glad of that." There was no triumph in the words. They just seemed to be a statement of facts. She looked across at the old man who was holding the flare of his lighter to the end of his cigar, "Do you mind if I sit? It is tiring standing."

The Professor nodded his head to indicate that he did not mind her taking a seat. She sat down beside me on the sofa, but for all that I felt someone might have placed a cushion beside me. My mind was a turmoil of fears and horrors.

"I had to kill Arthur," she continued, "for he remembered that Stella had pointed out the poisonous toadstools as we were picking them and had warned me against them and had told me how to distinguish them from the real mushrooms. As if I had not known already. After it was clear that Stella had been murdered, he remembered this, so I had to get rid of him. I had not made up my mind how to do it, but I took a chance that evening in the Underground and I succeeded. It was easy. I had to kill him, but it was not real, like killing Stella. I got no satisfaction out of it. I did not like Arthur, but I had no reason for killing him except that he was dangerous. He might have got me into trouble and I did not want to be in trouble. Once Stella was gone there was no reason why I should not succeed as I wanted to. I had to pretend that I was not too keen on Roger, but that was easy, for Max seemed to want to take me around, and he provided an excuse for not seeing too much of Roger. I knew that, in the end, I could get round Roger and then I would have been happy."

So, I said to myself, even your dreams were false, as false as dreams are. You were the cover for her heart and that was all. I felt lower than I think I have ever felt in my life. Someone once said that they felt so low that a snake could crawl over them without noticing them. That was a fair description of my feelings.

There seemed to be no end to the dreadful recital. Mary's voice went on.

"Of course," she said, "I was unfortunate. If there had not been a mix-up about the mushrooms which we had picked and those which Roger had bought in a shop, there would have been nothing but an accident. I thought I was quite safe. I did not see that there was anything that could go wrong. There wasn't anything to go wrong. I took no risk when I poured some of my mixture into Stella's plate. It was cold, but I knew that she would assume that the plate had got cold in being carried upstairs and that she wouldn't think of it. Douglas was so drunk that I knew he wouldn't notice how much I helped or what I did. It was pure bad luck that he remembered that he and Stella had eaten the shop mushrooms, and not the mushrooms from Linton. I could not have known that that was to happen.

There was no way in which I could have guarded against it happening. I was just unlucky. That's all."

"Uh-huh," the Professor grunted as he leaned forward to lower the ash from his cigar into the fireplace. "Ye were unlucky, but ye did yer best to make up for it. I wouldn't ha' thought ye were as quick witted as ye are. Ye showed yer quickness o' wit this evenin'."

"What do you mean?" she spoke slowly. I was as far from her as the Antipodes.

"Um," the old man blew out his lips, "I wouldn't think I'd need to tell ye that, eh?"

She looked at him blankly as if she did not know what he was talking about. He might have been lecturing on polyploidy[197] in wheat for all the intelligence she showed in her face.

He sighed heavily and scowled at the tip of his cigar. He hoisted himself out of his chair and lumbered over to the beer-barrel. He took down his quart mug and started to fill it. He turned his head over his shoulder and looked at her.

"Ye know what I mean," he grumbled, "I mean that ye showed yer quick wits in the way ye switched the dishes o' mushrooms an' *Amanita*. Ye may ha' known then that it was all up wi' ye, but ye were determined that ye'd make me pay for it."

Before I had time to digest the full meaning of this statement, she had risen to her feet and had thrown herself across the room at the Professor. I noticed that she was clutching a long sharp nail file in her hand. I was too stunned to move.

Harold Ironside did not seem to hurry. One moment he was sitting sunk in his chair and the next moment he was holding her. She seemed to be struggling violently, but he held her as easily as he would have held a wriggling mouse. Without effort, it seemed, he took the nail file out of her hand and let it fall to the ground. As quickly as she had flung herself at the Professor she seemed to relax again. Harold continued to hold her.

"Well," she said, and her voice was again expressionless, "I hope you suffer, and you," she pointed at me, "and you, Douglas. If it had not been for you I would have been happy. You can all do what you like but even the best doctors are apt to fail to cure poisoning by the Death Cap."

197 Polyploidy refers to an organism with more than two sets of chromsomes.

Professor Stubbs straightened up from his beer tap. He took a long pull at the mug and then he looked at her.

"My dear girl," he said slowly, "you didn't think that I was such a fool as to actually place the means o' poisonin' me in your hands. Both those dishes held nothin' but ordinary mushrooms."

CHAPTER NINETEEN

THE NATURE OF EXPLANATION

AFTER THAT even Harold had a job holding her. She put up a vicious fight. Considering how hurt Harold had been by Stella's death I thought that he handled her exceedingly gently. The Professor lifted the phone and rang the number of the police station. He usually makes a great parade of difficulty in handling the machine, but this evening he got through without any fuss or bother.

"Hey," he bawled into the mouthpiece, "that you Bishop? Well, ye can come along now. I got it all sewn up for ye."

I noticed that Alec Dolittle was apparently anxious to leave the room. He turned on one foot and then on the other. Finally, without excuse, he walked across and opened the door.

The door opened again and I assumed it was Alec returning. There was a sudden flash and a puff of acrid smoke. I turned to face the door fully. Alec stood there with a little man in a dirty trench coat and a battered trilby. Round the little man's neck there hung a camera.

For a moment the old man looked indignant at this invasion of his privacy. Then he beamed widely.

He glared round the room. "I'm thinkin'," he said "that most o' ye owe Mr. Dolittle an apology. Ye see the trouble about his behaviour which has been makin' ye suspect him, was that he's a journalist an' he's also a personal friend. Naturally, his instincts as a journalist ha' been in conflict wi' his instincts as a friend, and he's bin tryin' to be both at once, wi'out bein' particularly successful at bein' either. Now tonight he decided that he'd better let his instincts as a journalist get the upper hand an' ye'll all ha' noticed how much more at ease he has been since he made the decision. Now, Roger, I think ye should say ye're sorry."

Roger apologised with an extraordinary good grace. I was still looking at Harold holding Mary. She had ceased to struggle but he was holding her in readiness for a recrudescence of her violence.

"It's all right, Harold," she said meekly, "I won't fight any more. It's not worth it. Let me sit down."

He placed her in the large chair by the Professor's table and stood beside her. I could still look at her and feel thrilled by the sight of her beauty, but my heart no longer warmed me as I looked. The quick flush of love which had become so familiar had been turned off at the source. I thought of the way in which she had switched the dishes on the table. She could not have known how many people she would poison.

Her action seemed so pointless.

She must have realised that the Professor was sure who had done the murder, and it was difficult to see what she could have hoped to gain by killing about three or four people. Unless, of course, she had been so sure of herself that she had thought that the Professor had picked on someone else. I remembered how frequently I had told her of the old man's mistakes in which he had actually accused people of a murder before he had realised that he was wrong, and how I had stressed that these mistakes did not deter him in the least, but just urged him on until he found the right person.

That might have been it. With all the talk going on about Alec as the chief suspect, she might have made up her mind that she was safe for the moment, and that she would be safe until Alec had proved that he was not the murderer. That might have given her a few days in which we might all have died and then there would have been another inquest which would have pointed out how unsafe it was even for the expert to meddle with *Amanita phalloides*.

Arguing with herself in this way, and thinking very quickly indeed, she might have thought that her freedom was worth the risk of poisoning Roger, and then she might have had a second string to her thoughts, she might have been morally certain that a man so sensitive would not wish to take a meal of the things which had killed the girl he loved.

Provided that the Professor had made a mistake and had decided that Alec was the murderer, and that he had really served up a poisonous dish, she might very well have got away with it. But it was really too much of a long shot. Her action in changing the dishes showed the same quick decision as her sudden shove of Arthur Loftus on the platform.

Thinking back I could remember now that she had given me a sudden jerk just at the moment when the train came in and when Douglas had given us his excerpt from *Death's Jest Book*. I had not suspected her in the least. After all I had had my arm linked with hers and had had no reason to be suspicious.

She sat in her chair, as proud as Cleopatra and as fatal. Her eyes showed no sorrow for the deaths she had caused. I felt that inside there was no regret either, for anything but failure. If she had succeeded she might have become a popular actress and a respectable wife. She would have played both parts supremely well, but as she had failed I thought that she was playing the part of one who had lost all on the throw of a pair of dice and who was too puffed with pride to show emotion.

The Professor threw a couple of logs on to the fire. He turned his head towards Mary.

"Ye know, me dear," he said and his deep voice was surprisingly gentle. "They'll be here in a minute or two. Have ye anythin' ye'd like to say before they come? Anythin' ye want to say that ye don't want shouted around the court?"

Alec Dolittle chimed in. His photographer friend had departed. "I would like to say that, even though I am a journalist, I can hold my tongue."

The Professor nodded and looked again at Mary. "Well, me dear?" he said.

"No," she replied, "I have nothing to say. Nothing except that in the same circumstances I would do it again. It was only bad luck that beat me. I couldn't have known that things would go like that. How could I have known?"

She looked round the room, as if appealing for our agreement. No one seemed to be able to think of anything to say except Douglas, and, as usual, that was a quotation:

"The fault, dear Brutus, is not in our stars,
But in ourselves, that we are underlings."[198]

It was all very well for me to tell myself that Mary's behaviour and the things I had found out about her meant nothing to me. I could have gone on telling myself that till I was purple in the face but that still would not have made it true.

I got up and detached the sorely diminished brandy bottle from the

198 From *Julius Caesar* Act 1, Scene 2.

clutches of Douglas Newsome. I finished it off. It didn't have any effect on me. I still felt like hell.

The room seemed to me to be as empty of humanity as a vacuum receiver on an air-pump. No one seemed to feel quite as I did. I might easily have fallen to cursing at the top of my voice. I felt as hysterical as a nervous woman. The door bell rang loudly in the silence.

"Hey you, Max," the old man boomed, "Ull ye go an' let them in?"

I went. Having something to do, however trivial, was a help and I did my best to pull myself together as I went down the almost unending hallway. I opened the door with the feeling that I was opening the portal of hell.

"Good evening, Max," the Chief Inspector looked at me sleepily. His eyes were half closed in weariness. "How are you this evening?"

The question was rhetorical. I made no attempt to answer it. It must have been quite obvious to him exactly how I was feeling.

"John gave me a ring," he went on, "to tell me that he had solved his case. Is that true?"

"Yes," I replied dismally and led the way back towards the room. Behind the Chief Inspector there were other figures. I disowned any connection with them as I opened the door and announced the Chief Inspector.

The room gave me the impression that it was one of those interiors in the Victoria and Albert Museum which had suddenly been peopled by wax figures from Mme. Tussaud's. No one seemed to have moved an inch from where they had been when I had left the room. Even the appearance of the Bishop with his minions made no difference. In fact I felt that it was rather as if I had been Perseus entering the room carrying the Medusa's head, slung by its snaky locks.[199]

The Chief Inspector looked round the room slowly and wearily. "Well, John," he said in an expectant voice. I noticed that he was looking at both Roger and Alec Dolittle.

"Um," the old man stirred himself out of his brown study, "there's yer culprit."

He gestured towards Mary and I thought that his words and motion were too cruel to be borne. I felt as I had earlier. I could very nearly have risen to slap him. I looked at the Chief Inspector. He had pulled his eyes reluctantly away from his two suspects and was looking at Mary with

199 In Chapter 6 it is the Professor that is compared with Perseus.

complete surprise. I believe I have never seen his eyes so wide open.

"Yes," Mary spoke, and she got slowly to her feet. Her gestures were superb. I felt once more that I was watching a great actress. "I am your criminal." She did not slur her words. "I killed Stella Mortimer and Arthur Loftus and I am glad of it."

She walked slowly across to meet him. His eyelids slowly drooped towards his cheeks. He poured out the official formula.

"Mary Winstone, I arrest you," he had no warrant so he had to drop that out, "on the charge of having murdered Stella Mortimer and Arthur Loftus. It is my duty to warn you that anything you say will be taken down and may be used in evidence at your trial."

Mary paid no attention to the warning. "That's all right," she said, "I have admitted that I killed them. I wish it was all over."

I do not think that I was imagining a feeling in her voice when I felt that the last statement showed the only trace of emotion she had allowed herself since the Professor had made his statement accusing her.

Two of the Chief Inspector's underlings came forward. They fell in on each side of her and she walked out of the room between them. She did not turn her head to look at any of us. I think I felt hurt by this, for I had thought that she might, at least, make some sign towards me. Her exit was perfect from a theatrical point of view. It left us all quite speechless.

I heard the front door shut and I shuddered. I had been with the old man long enough to know about the dreadful wait for trial.

The Chief Inspector looked over at the old man. He then glanced at the bottle. It was as empty as it possibly could be. I had drained it. The Professor noticed the Bishop's glance and told me to fetch another bottle.

"Well, John," the Chief Inspector sat down, "what have you to say for yourself?"

"Me?" said the Professor, with a start of injured surprise, "what ha' I to say for meself? I ain't done nothin' that I ha' to explain."

The Bishop seemed slightly irritated. He took a sip of his brandy and helped himself to one of the old man's cigars. He lit it carefully and then leaned back comfortably. I could forgive him his offhand attitude. After all, what was he to Mary or Mary to him, to paraphrase one of Douglas's quotations.

"What I want to know, John," he was persistent, "was how you worked it out or whether it was, as usual, just some of your guesswork and bluff.

Which was it now?"

The old man grunted angrily, like an old scrub-bull. He snorted at the Bishop who remained unimpressed by his antics and merely repeated his question.

"Well," the Professor was curiously coy as if he was partly ashamed of himself, "ye see I got an odd sort o' mind. As soon as I got to know the figures in the case I realised that no one was suspectin' the one person who could ha' done the murder o' Stella Mortimer. I didn't much bother meself about the death o' Arthur Loftus when that happened, as it was quite obvious that any one o' those on the platform might ha' given him the necessary push. Why, the only witness ye got to the business in the Underground was an old bird who'd ha' sworn that it was young Max who did the deed. An' I may say, she wasn't so far from the truth at that. The girl was hangin' on his arm an' naturally she made him lurch when she gave Loftus the shove. He, bein' an innocent kinda soul, merely thought it was the crowd shovin' him and promptly forgot about it."

He lumbered across to refill his beer-mug and offered beer or brandy to those who wanted it. Douglas Newsome and I were the only people who stuck to brandy.

Once he was seated again he started to fill his pipe. If he'd had buttoned boots I guess he'd have unbuttoned them. There was that kind of unbuttoned look about him.

"Ye, see, Reggie, if ye hadn't let yer mind get led away by yer mistrust o' me detective ability, ye'd ha' realised at once that Mary Winstone was the obvious person to ha' committed the murder. Ye wanted to go on believin' that it was an accident, an' ye also wanted to believe that Loftus's death was accidental. It's a dam' sight more difficult to do anythin' wi' a murder that has got past the coroner an' bin dismissed as an accident. I knew that an' I knew that you were dam' well certain to make a goddam fool o' yerself, an' to try and bury it."

The Chief Inspector looked up from his contemplation of the excellent quality of his cigar.

"That's hardly fair, John," he said mildly. "You know that I always take action when I see an opportunity for it. The trouble in this case is that there was no avenue through which I could take action."

"All right, all right," the old man gestured benevolently, "I'll absolve ye from the charge o' neglectin' to do yer duty, but ye want to know how I worked it out an' that's a part o' the business. Ye see," he beamed fiercely, "I got so dam' hoppin' mad that I determined that I'd solve the thunderin' business wi'out the help o' the blinkin' coppers. It ain't easy to work wi'out 'em, but I just kinda set my brain to work an' before I knew where I was the figure o' Mary Winstone was standin' out clear as the most obvious suspect. Ye see, she was clever, an' she thought that the fact that she admitted pickin' fungi wi' the Mortimer girl would act as a kinda alibi for her, an' she was dam' well right. No one, except me, gave her a second thought. Me, I got a nasty mind, an' I started to think what there was that could ha' prompted her to want to kill her friend. I got bits and pieces all over the place, some o' them from Loftus who was obviously holdin' back somethin' an' some o' them from Max. He's a good reporter, he is, an' can remember mostly what people say in his presence."

I was by this time feeling slightly the worse for the drink I had taken. To begin with I had felt that all the brandy in the world could have no effect on me, but it was gradually creeping up on my mind. I wanted to go and sleep more than I wanted to do anything else, and I hoped that when I slept that I would be untroubled by dreams.

The old man was now well into his stride. He glanced at me once or twice as he spoke and I knew that he was trying to suggest that I kept myself in check. There was no need for him to do that, for I had myself so firmly worked in that it would have taken an oxygen blow-pipe to release me.

"Uh-huh," he was rumbling on, "once I got me idea that she needed a bit o' investigation, the rest was simple. I just went down to where she was actin' in the country an' started maulin' around her room. I found that little pot," he again produced it, "an' I guessed it didn't hold sandwich spread or face cream, so I brought it back wi' me. There are traces o' the spores o' *Amanita phalloides* in it. All the same, the girl had bin clever enough to let us know that her friend Stella was interested in the subject o' the wild foods o' Britain an' the jar might well ha' bin left over from one of her experiments. She might ha' cooked some o' the fungi to see how different it looked from the ordinary field mushroom. If Mary Winstone had bin able to brazen that out, I had nothin' tangible in the way o' proof, tho' me head was as full o' doubts as a hive is o' bees. But then, ye see, Reggie, I arranged a little performance for this evenin'. I served up two dishes, which look identical, an' I announced that one o' 'em was full o' field mushrooms, *Psalliota campestris*, while the other, which looked indistinguishable, was the

Death Cap. Then, kinda accidental like done a purpose, the lights fused. During the time the room was in darkness, Mary Winstone, whom I'd placed conveniently near, switched the dishes."

"My God," the Chief Inspector looked startled, "you might have been poisoned, John."

The Professor looked at him with benevolent pity. He shook his head sadly with the air of one who despairs of humanity.

"Ye're as bad as the girl, Reggie," he exploded, "d'ye really think that I'd serve up a plate full of *Amanita phalloides*? If ye do ye're a blinkin' thunderin' fool and deserve to be poisoned. O' course the two dishes were identical – they were identical in their contents too. They both held nothin' beyond ordinary mushrooms. I did a bit of cookery meself this afternoon an' I found that ye wouldn't know the difference when cooked, so I felt I could go ahead wi' me bluff. Apart from that, I know the dishes apart. One o' 'em has a kinda dent in the edge an' I knew that was the one I was callin' mushrooms. Well, at the start o' me little performance, that one was on me right, an' after Max had dealt wi' the fuse, it ended upon me left. So I knew then that I was certain to be right. The one thing that made me absolutely positive was that the only other person who could have changed the dishes was Douglas Newsome, and he was the only one of me visitors who accepted the mushrooms."

Hearing his name mentioned Douglas looked sadly over the edge of his brandy glass. He did not seem to find much comfort in life. He looked at Professor Stubbs rather wistfully.

"Well you see, sir," he said tentatively, "you weren't quite right. I knew that Mary had changed the dishes. She has a little watch with luminous dabs on the hands and I saw that as she did it."

If you had suddenly kicked the Professor in the stomach you could not have surprised him more.

"You knew that she changed the dishes," he demanded, "and yet you accepted a helping o' what ye thought might be a deadly poison fungi. What on earth were you thinking of?"

"Oh," Douglas was vague, "I didn't think much. I just assumed that you were playing a game, and if you weren't and I really was poisoned it seemed to me that it would be an experience."

He buried himself once more in his brandy glass, oblivious to the looks which all those in the room cast at him. All I could think was that he was an extraordinary young man. His statement had put the old man out of step in a way that nothing else could have done. The rest of the story was told in a rather flat way. I felt relieved by this, as I did not feel that I could have stood much more of the Professor gloating over the cleverness that he had exercised at the expense of Mary. It was no use me telling myself that I had made a fool of myself. I knew that, but it did not lessen the hurt which I had sustained. The one thing which I felt I could not forgive was that she had hoped that we would suffer. I might have forgiven her for hoping that the old man and Douglas would suffer, but I could not see why she had included me in her wishes. I had never done anything to hurt her, and, in fact, she must have found me quite helpful as a source of information as to the old man's actions and suspicions. The fact that I had been wrongly informed about them myself was not my fault, and I couldn't blame the Professor for it either. It was true that if he had told me his ideas I might have refrained from passing the information on to Mary, but it was equally true that I might have given away a good deal in my attitude.

I kept on trying to think of reasons why I should be angry with the old man, but I couldn't find any. He had certainly hurt me, but then I was bound to be hurt in any case. Mary, whom I had thought fond of me, had only been using me as a kind of rather dumb stalking-horse to let her approach Roger. She'd have ditched me pretty quickly as soon as she felt that it was safe to do so.

"In fact, John," the Bishop was speaking and he was as bland as a pontiff, "you just muddled your way through in the usual manner. You tried out one or two experiments, based on your guesses and you found they worked out, so you just assumed that you were right. It was pure luck, as it turned out, that you were able to sting the girl into confessing in the presence of witnesses. I very much doubt whether there is sufficient evidence in all that you say to prove the case in court without that. Pure luck, John, that's what it is!"

Professor Stubbs was indignant and deeply wounded. He appealed to the heavens to fall on Chief Inspector Reginald F. Bishop and destroy him for his ingratitude.

"Me," he bellowed, "I got the scientific mind. I approach things in the scientific manner an' I get me results which are either demonstrably right or else demonstrably wrong. I work out the only way a thin' can ha' happened, an' then this dunderheaded dolt has the blinkin' nerve to come an' tell me that it's all luck. Bah! Phooey!"

The Chief Inspector looked down the side of his cigar and sighed comfortably. He seemed to be very pleased with himself. He looked like a large Persian cat which had just had a pint of double cream.

"Ah, well, John," he said easily, "so long as you can go on believing that you'll be a happy man. If I can't but think that you are one of the luckiest men alive, that's my own opinion and it won't alter your view of yourself."

Professor Stubbs was, for once in his life, speechless with the force of his indignation.

CHAPTER TWENTY

IF THE CAP FITS

I COULD not say that I found life during the next few weeks very happy. The Professor made me work harder than he'd ever made me work before. I started in as soon as I got up in the morning and when the night came I was so tired that I went straight to sleep.

The only thing that could be said for this slave-driving was that at last the *History of Botany* began to take shape. About whether it would retain that shape I was not sanguine. I had seen things begin to jell before and I had seen Professor Stubbs set to work to melt them. He has a genius for diffuseness.

The day before Mary's trial he was up and dressed before me. He had done all the household chores. Over breakfast he sat silent. I thought he was thinking out the programme of work for the coming day.

Suddenly he looked out of his coffee-cup and glared at me. "Ye're look-ing tired, Max," he announced solicitously. I was surprised at this attention from him, for I did not think he noticed whether I was alive or dead when he was engaged on a piece of work.

I admitted that, indeed, I felt tired.

"Hum," he said, "I was thinkin' it was time ye had a holiday an' I booked a room at a pub near Henley[200] for ye. I'll run ye down there to-day, an' I'll collect ye in a week's time. Mind ye, Max, this don't count as the holiday ye're always goin' to have. Ye can ha' that after, if ye want it. This is a bonus."

I argued with him, pointing out that there was a great deal of work to do and that, anyhow, I was quite likely to be called as a witness at Mary's trial. He wouldn't accept my arguments. He demanded how I thought he had managed before I came along. (I sometimes wonder how he did.)

200 Henley-on-Thames is a town in South Oxfordshire famous for rowing and its Royal Regatta.

Finally he pulled his trump card. "I fixed it so's ye won't be called at the trial," he announced, "so there's no need for ye to stay in town for that. It's no use yer arguin', boy, I won't take no from ye. Get on upstairs an' pack yer bag."

I might as well have tried to oppose a bulldozer. I gave way and went and packed my things. I put a bundle of books on the back seat of the Bentley and we roared off. I could not say that the journey was a restful prelude to a holiday. The old man's driving frightens the guts out of me.

The pub was very pleasant though and the old man persuaded the land-lady that I was suffering from overwork and should be coddled. I had hardly time to think before he had roared off back to town, and I had been more or less forcibly pushed into bed. That night, the first for several weeks, I slept without dreaming.

In the morning I decided that I would take myself for a walk. I strolled along the road until I came to a large field beside an oak wood. I climbed over the hedge and started down the side of the wood. There was a beau-tiful autumn sun shining among the yellowed leaves of the trees. I felt thoroughly rested in my body if not in my mind.

Looking down at my feet I saw, pushing its ugly head through the white volva, the olive green of *Amanita phalloides*. The Death Cap, I thought, and I remembered another Death Cap, and a wigged man with a nosegay.

I placed my foot upon the fungus and squashed it to a pulp, then I turned and went back towards the road.

Colophon

Printed and bound in Great Britain by Berforts in Hastings, East Sussex on 90gsm bookwove.

Book design, layout and typesetting by Omnis Partners, Cumbernauld, Scotland.

Typefaces: Adobe Caslon Pro (William Caslon, Carol Twombly), Shaker (Jeremy Tankard) and Quadraat Sans (Fred Smeijers).